T0249888

Security Implementation in Internet of Medical Things

Security implementation is crucial in the Internet of Medical Things (IoMT) as it ensures the protection of sensitive medical data and prevents unauthorized access or manipulation of devices and systems. This book covers different aspects of security implementations and challenges in IoMT and aims to bring researchers together to contribute their findings to recommend new methodologies and feasible solutions for implementing security and novel architectures in artificial intelligence, machine learning, and data science in the field of healthcare and IoT.

The IoMT includes a wide range of connected medical devices and systems, such as wearable devices, medical sensors, and electronic health records, that collect, store, and share sensitive medical information. Without proper security measures, this information could be compromised, leading to serious privacy breaches, financial fraud, and even physical harm to patients.

Security Implementation in Internet of Medical Things

Edited by
Luxmi Sapra
Varun Sapra
Akashdeep Bhardwaj

CRC Press
Taylor & Francis Group
Boca Raton London New York

CRC Press is an imprint of the
Taylor & Francis Group, an **informa** business

First edition published 2024
by CRC Press
6000 Broken Sound Parkway NW, Suite 300, Boca Raton, FL 33487-2742

and by CRC Press
4 Park Square, Milton Park, Abingdon, Oxon, OX14 4RN

CRC Press is an imprint of Taylor & Francis Group, LLC

ISBN: 978-1-032-21603-4 (hbk)
ISBN: 978-1-032-21606-5 (pbk)
ISBN: 978-1-003-26916-8 (ebk)

DOI: 10.1201/9781003269168

Typeset in Caslon
by MPS Limited, Dehradun

Contents

About the Editors

 **Dr. Luxmi Sapra** is working as an associate professor at Graphic Era Hill University, Dehradun, India. She has received her doctorate in computer science and engineering from NorthCap University and received her master's in technology from MDU, Rohtak. India. She has approximately 18 years of research and teaching experience. She has to her credit more than 30 publications in reputed journals and conferences including Elsevier, Springer, and IEEE. She is also a reviewer of various international journals. She also received 3AI Pinnacle Award for Women in AI and Analytics in 2020 and was awarded 4th Himalayi Nari Shakti Samman-2022 on the occasion of Women's Day 8th March 2022 at DIT University, Dehradun. Her research areas include cybersecurity, machine learning, artificial intelligence, and healthcare.

Dr. Varun Sapra is presently associated with the School of Computer Science, University of Petroleum and Energy Studies, Dehradun, India. He is an accomplished academic professional with 18 years of experience in both academia and industry. His experience is a blend of both industry and academia. Before joining academics, he was in the corporate sector and worked in companies like Cupid Software, WebOpac Applications, CMA, and many more. Dr. Varun received a PhD in computer science and M.Tech in software engineering. He has to his credit more than 25 publications in peer-reviewed international journals and conferences and has published several copyrights, patents, research papers, and edited books, and chapters in international journals and publications. His research areas include machine learning, decision support systems, case-based reasoning, and self-organizing maps.

Dr. Akashdeep Bhardwaj is working as a professor (cybersecurity and digital forensics) at the University of Petroleum & Energy Studies (UPES), Dehradun, India. An eminent IT industry expert with over 27 years of experience in areas such as cybersecurity, digital forensics, and IT management operations, Dr. Akashdeep now mentors graduate, masters, and doctoral students and leads several IT security projects. Dr. Akashdeep has a post-doctoral from Saudi Arabia, PhD in computer science, postgraduate diploma in management (equivalent to MBA), and an engineering degree in computer science. Dr. Akashdeep has published several copyrights, patents, research papers, authored and edited books, and chapters in international journals and publishers. Dr. Akashdeep worked as a technology leader for various multinational organizations during his time in the IT industry. Dr. Akashdeep is certified in cybersecurity, compliance audits, information security, Microsoft, Cisco, and VMware technologies.

Contributors

Prachi Ahlawat
Department of Computer
  Science & Engineering
The NorthCap University
Gurugram, India

Aparna Bannore
SIES Graduate School of
  Technology
Nerul, Navi Mumbai, India

Parijat Bhowmick
Department of Electrical and
  Electronics and
  Communication Engineering
IIT Guwahati, Assam, India

A. S. N. Chakravarthy
CSE Dept.
JNTUK Kakinada, India

Rishiraj Singh Chhabra
Vellore Institute of Technology
Tamil Nadu, India

Sima Das
Department of Computer
  Science and Engineering
Bengal College of Engineering
  and Technology
Durgapur, West Bengal, India

Samrah Butool Faridi
Era University
Lucknow, India

Nafees Akhter Farooqui
BBD University
Lucknow, India

Nimay Chandra Giri
Department of Electronics and
  Communication Engineering
  and Centre for Renewable
  Energy and Environment
Centurion University of
  Technology and Management
Odisha, India

K. Jhajharia
Manipal University Jaipur
India

Sumit Kumar Jindal
Vellore Institute of Technology
Tamil Nadu, India

Divyansh Khandelwal
Vellore Institute of Technology
Tamil Nadu, India

Sumit Kumar
Department of Computer
  Science & Engineering
The NorthCap University
Gurugram, India

R. Malthiyar
Manipal University Jaipur
India

Kaushik Mazumdar
Department of Electronics and
  Communication Engineering
IIT Dhanbad (ISM) India

Ritika Mehra
Dev Bhoomi Uttarakhand
  University
Dehradun, India

Shilpa Mehta
Department of Electrical and
  Electronic Engineering
Auckland University of
  Technology
New Zealand

Divya Pant
Plant Science Department
Pennsylvania State University
University Park
State College
Pennsylvania, U.S.A.

Rachana Y. Patil
Pimpri Chinchwad College of
  Engineering
Pune, Maharashtra, India

Yogesh H. Patil
Dr. D. Y. Patil Institute of
  Technology
Pune, Maharashtra, India

Sameeka Saini
Dev Bhoomi Uttarakhand
  University
Dehradun, India

Himanshu Tiwari
Department of Agronomy
Sardar Vallabhbhai Patel
  University of Agriculture and
  Technology
Meerut, India

Manas Kumar Yogi
CSE Dept.
Pragati Engineering
India

1

IoT

An Emerging Boon in Today's Healthcare Industry

SAMEEKA SAINI

*Dev Bhoomi Uttarakhand
University, Dehradun, India*

Abstract

Due to a rapid increase in technologies and smart devices, our way of living and working is becoming easy and fascinating day by day. Various emerging technologies have been invented in various sectors by keeping in mind the factors such as ease of access, accuracy, safety, and a lot more. One of the latest is IoT: Internet of Things. IoT is basically the interconnection of various physical devices with the help of the internet for sharing data or resources. IoT is gaining popularity because of its advantages in various sectors such as industry auto-mation, healthcare, smart homes, smart cities, agriculture, etc. With the help of IoT, various health monitoring devices and techniques have been invented that can allow a patient to be in touch with a doctor every time and their body's reading such as BP, hemoglobin, heart rate, stress rate, etc. can be recorded automatically after a fixed interval.

Smartwatches, wigs, glasses, and gloves are a few examples of smart wearables. Smart contact lenses capture and process the data with the blink of one's eye. Apart from this, it can monitor the blood glucose level for diabetic patients with the help of tears in the eye. Because of IoT, one manage the patient's information of their body readings, bed availability, doctor availability, medicine avail-abilities, and a lot. Moreover, the only limitation of IoT is over-come by BIoT i.e., blockchain IoT. In this chapter, we will cover

DOI: 10.1201/9781003269168-1

the basics of IoT in healthcare, examples of various wearables invented using IoT in healthcare, the various healthcare areas where IoT is gaining popularity, and the research work that has been done in healthcare using IoT along with their comparisons.

1.1 Introduction

Earlier interconnection of a few computers was designed for communication. The main aim was to share or access scarce and expensive computing resources. After the development of TCP/IP and other protocols, tremendous growth was seen in the global network with the help of the internet. Since then, we are observing continuous change and growth in the field of networking. From the advancement of mobile phones, touch screens, and lightweight laptops to the World Wide Web, social networking websites, and numerous chatting applications, the main focus is on connecting with people for communication and sharing of data [1].

The internet was itself so fascinating because we were able to connect to different people and communicate with them so easily over a long distance also. As time evolved, the internet gained popularity by increasing its application areas in various sectors. The internet is not restricted to sending emails and writing blogs; it has extended its services in various areas such as online booking of movies ticket, bus tickets, flight tickets, and train tickets; online booking of food and seats in restaurants, for example, zomato and swiggy; online booking of medicines such as netmeds; electronic money payments; and money transfers, for example, Bhim, Paytm, phone pay, etc.; online payments of electricity bills; online shopping; for example, Flipkart, Amazon, Myntra, etc.; online teaching and learning like unacademy; online listening music like Wynk music; watching online movies on OTT platforms such as Netflix, etc. have made our life easy. Now we are having smart AI machines and using this technology in making life easier such as Alexa, Siri, Google assistant, Tesla (the smart self-driving car), and a lot more. The evolution of the internet is shown in Figure 1.1.

The initial phase was of connecting computers or devices with each other to form a network and in the second phase, WWW came into

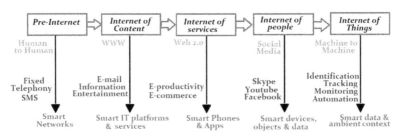

Figure 1.1 Evolution of Internet and IoT.

existence where several computers were connected as a web. Then came the mobile internet in web 2.0 where people used to connect to the web using mobile phones and can access social networking websites for communicating. Finally, the current phase evolved i.e., the era of IoT.

IoT is the Internet of Things; the term is used to define the interconnection of millions of devices or computers connected with the internet for communication purposes. With IoT, it is possible to connect people with things anywhere, anytime, any place with anyone. This concept can be summarized by defining two important features, i.e., automation and connectivity. The evolution in IoT gives rise to many terms such as IIoT (Industrial Internet of Things), BIoT (Blockchain Internet of Things), SIoT (Social Internet of Things), MIoT (Military Internet of Things), etc. IoT is gaining popularity because of the following reasons:

1. IoT has a lower operating cost as compared with other technologies.
2. It offers higher employee productivity.
3. It provides better customer experience.
4. New consumer insights.
5. IoT enhances the data collection.
6. Innovation, etc.

IoT consists of basically four component sensors or actuators that are able to emit-accept-process data, devices, gateway, or networks to transfer the data and cloud for storage. Figure 1.2 shows the components of IoT.

With the help of the internet, we can easily send or receive data as the internet is a collection of various inter-connected networks. This feature makes the internet or device better and smart. The connected

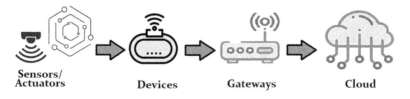

Figure 1.2 Components of IoT.

or embedded sensors in the device help to collect data that can be analyzed later to extract some important information from that data. These IoT effective platforms can identify exactly what information is useful and what can be ignored. The best example of IoT automation is the smart home, which consists of smart windows, smart doors, smart kitchens, smart television, smart AC, and smart refrigeration that can be accessed by one's cell phone through Wi-Fi or other wireless technologies, etc. Some examples of a smart home are Insteon Hub Pro, Google Home, Wink Hub, etc.

Being the latest technology IoT has a wide area of application in various sectors. IoT application areas are smart homes, smart cities, smart energy, smart architecture, smart agriculture, IoT automotive, smart retail, wearables, gaming, AR (augmented reality), and VR (virtual reality), etc. IoT provides businesses and people with a better perception of and control over objects and environments that are currently afar of the grasp of the internet. Figure 1.3 shows the

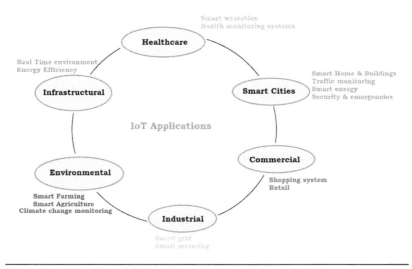

Figure 1.3 Applications of IoT.

various applications of IoT i.e., healthcare, transportation, commercial, and a lot more.

1. Healthcare: Earlier, the interaction between patient and doctor was just through visits, texts, and telecommunication, but after the arrival of IoT technology we have empowered doctors to give superlative care by remote monitoring the patients. As of now, we have a remote monitoring system that can collect metrics such as heart rate, BP, etc. of the remotely located patient and send the report to the doctor for examining the patient. In glucose monitoring, the diabetic patient's information is remotely transferred to the doctor for regular checking up of the patient. In the heart rate monitoring system, the periodic heart rate measured report is shared with the doctor. Apart from these, we have connected inhalers, ingestible sensors, connected contact lenses, mood monitoring systems, robotic surgery, etc. [2].

   Smart devices in healthcare have made a boon in the medical sector. Wearables are electronic-enabled devices used to track the patient's real-time health data including blood pressure, heart rate, pulse rate, glucose level, etc. Mhealth is mobile healthcare, which is a technology where doctors and patients can interact face-to-face but remotely [3]. Telehealth, telemedicine, and remote patient health checking have supported patients' lives in the case of medical tragedies like asthma attacks, heart failure, and diabetes. The usage of wearables (WIoT) can bring efficiency and optimization to the application, improve the quality of life, and rise production or security. Smartwatches, wristbands, eye wears, headsets, earbuds, body straps, and foot and hand-worn devices are examples of some smart wearables [4]. The research work done in this area to now works in the area of wearable IoT devices using unlicensed little-range communication technology such as Bluetooth, and Wi-Fi, primarily to monitor the patient's health, activity, location, etc. With the help of these smart devices, not only the patients are getting advantages but also it is a boon for sports persons. For example, the smartwatch helps and brings an abundance of opportunities in enhancing their proficiency by creating a setting in which athletes can get better training and coaches can examine injuries or discover metrics on player performance, etc. [4]. Figure 1.4 shows healthcare applications using IoT.

2. Smart Homes: Since we can control the surrounding devices with the help of a single touch of a screen on our smartphones, our life has become convenient and fast. In the smart home, we can control, monitor, and manage the systems such as heat, light, temperature, etc. with the help of smartphones and sensors. Figure 1.5 shows the smart home with smart solar panels, air conditioning system control, video game

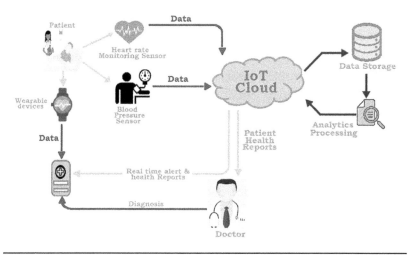

Figure 1.4   Healthcare operation using IoT.

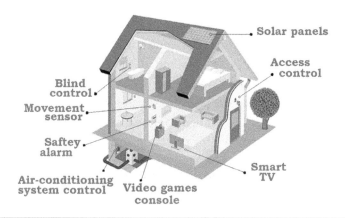

Figure 1.5   A smart home.

console, movement system, safety alarm, and a smart access entry control on the entrance of the home [5].

3. Smart cities: There are many ways to define a smart city. A smart city is a city in which the resources are used optimally and efficiently for connecting people with technology. A smart city is a combination of automation, machine learning, and IoT. For example, a smart parking system that helps drivers to find space and allow digital payment, smart traffic management to monitor traffic and reduce congestion without the help of traffic police present there, and smart energy conservation that controls the streetlights that dim when roads are empty, smart buildings, etc. are some technologies whose existence makes a city smart. Figure 1.6 shows a glimpse of a smart city [6].

4. Smart Energy: IoT is making a very grateful impact on electrical industries also. In 2012, the very first-time smart energy system word was used. Smart energy is the process of using devices for home appliances or industries or automobiles that are energy efficient i.e., uses less energy and also keep the environment clean and green with less pollution. Making houses insulated, having a smart meter, having solar panels, etc. are some of the examples that contribute toward smart energy in any house [7]. Figure 1.7 shows the smart energy.

Apart from the above list, the applications of IoT devices are numerous as smart vehicles in automobile areas, smart farming, smart agriculture,

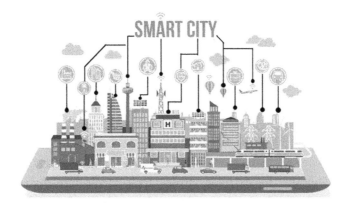

Figure 1.6 Smart cities using IoT.

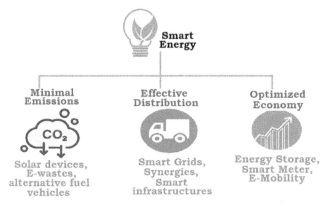

Figure 1.7   Smart energy using IoT.

smart grid and monitoring in industries, and smart shopping and retailing. But the major impact can be seen in the healthcare industry.

1.2 IoT Technology Used in Healthcare Sector

The assimilation of IoT has regulated the excellence of life in numerous methods. It has provided novel visions, efficiency, and cost-effectiveness in various application areas. With the help of IoT technologies, we can get a better and more early accurate diagnosis of severe disease at the right time. IoT has transformed hospitals into smart hospitals. The dissatisfaction among patients regarding the long waiting queue, overloaded and busy doctors and nurses, an immense load of paperwork, unavailability of beds and medicines, etc. can be handled by and with the help of IoT technologies. The paperwork or registration can be replaced by an automated centralized database that keeps the record of all individual patients who ever visited the hospital. Online tracking of the availability of respective doctors, medical equipment, beds, and medicines can be done with the help of smartphones. It is more efficient as a normal ill person can also concern or get diagnosed by the doctors remotely or online. For example, if a person is having a normal cough and cold, he can consult a doctor online, and there is no need to visit the hospital in person. Numerous online healthcare applications are available for daily use; for example, fitness apps, medication management apps, sleep tracking apps, pregnancy monitoring apps, health monitoring apps, and many more.

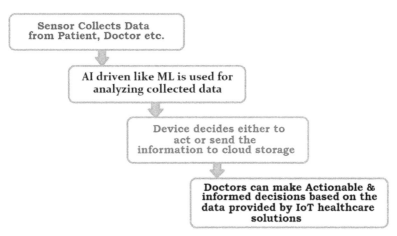

Figure 1.8 Process of healthcare IoT.

A wide variety of recent technologies are used with IoT such as artificial intelligence, machine learning and deep learning, sensors and RFIDs (radio frequency identification), fog computing, etc. sensors and RFID are used for sensing the data and AI (artificial intelligence), ML (machine language), and DL (deep learning) can be used to analyze the stored data. Apart from all these, an important technology that is gaining popularity is blockchain, which can be combined with IoT to form BIoT. BIoT is more secure than simple IoT. Blockchain plays an important role and provides security in storing, sharing, and retrieving remotely collected biomedical data. Blockchain's immutability and transparency can be used in healthcare insurance claims [8].

In the medical field, the revolution has been created by wireless healthcare monitoring systems using IoT [9]. Figure 1.8 depicts how IoT helps in the healthcare sector. Firstly, the data is collected from the patient's body with the help of sensors. That data is stored in the cloud, or it can be sent to a doctor's device for analysis with the help of artificial intelligence and machine learning technologies. Finally, the doctor can decide based on analyzed data or can confirm the disease and start the treatment.

The following technologies have been used in the healthcare sector with the help of IoT:

1. Remote health monitoring: Using IoT, we can capture the health data of a patient, store it in the cloud, and use that

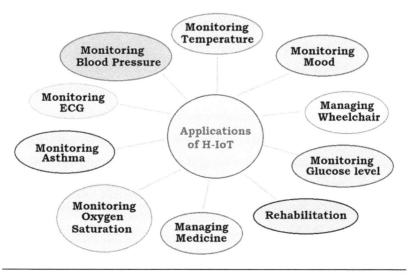

Figure 1.9 Applications of HIoT.

data later for analyzing a patient's health, prescribing medicines, etc. As in the COVID-19 lockdown situation, this
technique was a boon for medical patients. Patients were
consulting doctors over the internet remotely and doctors were
able to diagnose them just because of their medical history and
data that were captured and stored on the cloud with the help
of sensors. In remote monitoring, we can consider respiratory
monitor, heart rate monitoring, insulin/glucose monitoring,
pulse rate monitoring, BP monitoring, etc. Figure 1.9 shows
the applications of healthcare IoT (HIoT).

2. Body Wearables: These are devices or biosensors for monitoring and self-assistance. Smart wearables such as smartwatches, smart lenses, smart audible aids, etc. are used to
monitor and record the various data of any patient's body.
They can be used to make decisions and precautions on
medical terms and can monitor health. Examples include
fitness trackers, heart rate trackers, etc.

3. Customized patient medicine pervading: The medicine of a
patient can be customized and automated using the patient's
medical data. Smart wearables can be used with IoT; for example, IoT-based asthma inhalers, etc. The request and supply
of medicine prescriptions can be automated and customized.

4. Maintenance of medical equipment: The medical equipment and tools can be effectively maintained so that we can save money and lives. Collected data, faulty reports, and track of usage help in maintaining medical equipment.

5. Medical asset management: Imagine you are severly injured or ill and there is no bed available for you. In such situations, if this type of information is available beforehand, it will help the patient to go to another hospital or search for one that has bed availability. Bed availability, doctor availability, medical equipment, and other assets must be trackable earlier to respond to emergencies, cost reduction, and other medical care experiences, which is possible through smart IoT devices.

6. Clinical Care: The IoT manages the information in the hospital such as availability of doctors, availability of appointments, availability of medicines, availability of equipment, medical record identification, testing product identification, illness recognition, etc. Using RFID technology, the data is sensed and recorded for doctors remotely.

1.3 The Smart Wearables for Healthcare

Smart wearables are those devices that are used to collect the sensed data of a person to analyze their health or other parameters. Different wearables that are developed and used by humans include smart belts, smartwatches, smart clothing, smart glasses, smart footwear, activity trackers, tattoo, ingestible, jewelry, medical wearables, smart headphones, etc. They gather information and then analyze it to make some decisions [10]. The smart wearables can be categorized as:

1. Tracking and localization: These types of smart devices are used to track humans or animals at some location. For example, a mother can wear this device on their small child to track his moment when she is not near him. Also, reviewing the path tour of a bird, discovering a locality of a senior citizen in a care-home facility, analyzing the movement of people who are attending any event, and tracking pets are some of the common examples.

2. Safety and Welfare: These types of wearables are best for women. For example, women working late at night at some place and returning home will help them in case of any type of emergency. Or this type of device can be used in laboratories or mines to ensure the health of doctors/nurses or workers against harmful air quality data.

3. Health: Wearables have created magic for patients. Wearables help to sense the heart rate for a heart attack vulnerable person, pulse rate, for a person vulnerable to dizziness, fainting, chest pain, etc., glucose level for diabetic patients, pulse oximeter sensors for measuring blood oxygen in a patient, blood pressure measurement for weak heart patients, body temperature measurement for measuring fever, heat stroke, etc., and respiration rate for asthma patients.

4. Activity Identification: Smart wearables are also used in monitoring daily activities. The physical activities include tracking daily routines and movements of the body such as walking, jumping, jogging, sleeping, running, stairs climbing, bending at the waist, moments of arms, bending knees, etc. Also, it recognizes static postures such as sitting, relaxing, standing still, laying down, etc. As an example, we can say that Fitbit is a smartwatch that monitors the daily activity of the wearer. The Fitbit can be synchronized with smartphones and on that, we can see the various health factors.

5. Sports: These wearables are worn by athletes during sports activities to record so that athletes can improve his/her performance. The wearable helps athletes to improve their performance as they get real-time feedback on their performance. The existence method senses and records the data in four states; Figure 1.10 shows the four stages used in sports wearables. It starts with pre-processing of the sensed data, and then feature extraction is done in two ways, either structural or statistical. The next following stage is the removal of redundant and inappropriate information and after this, finally, classification is done based on the pattern observed.

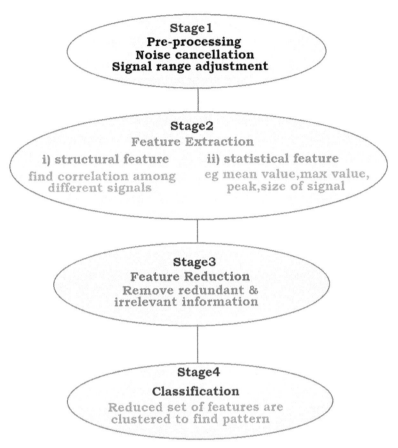

Figure 1.10 Stages of sports wearables.

Other smart wearables include hearables, ingestible sensors, mood-ables, computer vision technology, healthcare charting, smart video pills, smartwatches, smart lenses, etc.

Hearables are the advancement of headphones and wearables that consist of sensors, Bluetooth, speakers, and microphones. The hearables are used for heart rate monitoring, pulse monitoring, oxygen saturation, blood pressure, entertainment, guidance, and cloud-based communication. They help in better listening as well as listening of good sound quality audio or songs. Ingestible sensors are the pill-size electronic devices that are swallowed by patients. They are coated with zinc, copper, magnesium, or silicon that can measure body activity, heart rate, blood pressure, etc. They get their power from the zinc that emits ions into the stomach of humans. These are used to accomplish pill endoscopy that senses the image of the internal part of the patient to distant observing application software mounted in hospital systems [11]. Moodables are still in development that will help in studying the brain waves of humans, which will help in deciding the mood, level of mood swings, stress level, etc. of the patient. The smart pills or smart video pills are mini capsules that are swallowed by the patient and the recording is sent to the belt or device that is worn on the patient's body. For example, PillCam captures photos of the inside of a patient so that it can diagnose various diseases such as measurement of pH, pressure, temperature, etc.

A smartwatch is a wearable wristwatch that shows time and also some health factors. The smartwatch examples are Fitbit and Apple watches that can sync with your smartphone and can measure your daily physical activities [12]. One can wear them in daily life to access their smartphones or can measure their stress level, calories burnt, and heart rate [13]. Smart lenses are soft contact lens that provide minimum irritation to the eye and the wearer's view is not obstructed because these are prepared of translucent nanomaterials. The wearer's tears are collected in this lens by natural means such as blinking of the eyes or normal secretion of tears to assess various parameters such as glucose, cholesterol, sodium ions, and potassium ions [14]. Smart jewelry is also a kind of smart wearable that not only helps in medical examination but can also be used as an emergency device to contact police in case of sexual assault on any woman [15]. In [16] depicted the comparison of various smart wearables using machine learning. Other than these, there are smart clothes, smart headbands, smart wrist worn, wearable cameras, body sensors, etc. Some wearables are used by users, and some are still under development.

Although smart wearables are widely used by patients, athletes, and normal people, they offer various advantages as we have seen above. But they also face some major challenges, such as:

1. Safety and security: The sensor nodes are attached to the various human body parts such as the chest, hands, earlobes, etc. that radiates harmful radiofrequency that can have a negative impact on one's health. Also, wearing the devices for a long time can cause skin rashes or irritation or allergies.

Since these devices are small in size and lightweight, they don't have complex security features on them. The data that is sensed by these devices are then transferred to some cloud storage that can be breached or hacked by any attacker, making these smart devices less secure. Various types of active and passive attacks are possible during the transmission of data or while they are stored in the cloud.

2. Wearability: The wearable devices should be comfortable for wearing. They should be lightweight and meanwhile should be designed in a way that they should be comfortable in wearing and should not disturb normal activities. Also, they should be protected from water and sweat for their effective work.

3. Power Consumption: To operate these devices for a long duration, a continuous power supply is needed without replacement or charging of the battery. Some low-power usage system techniques were discussed in [17] such as micro-electric, thermoelectric, piezoelectric, photoelectric, etc. Solar energy is considered the best, but has only one problem, it is limited to daytime only.

4. Data Resolution: The devices are too small in size and are lightweight; the data sensed and captured are of really low resolution as compared to the non-wearable devices.

5. Confidentiality: The wearable device senses the data and communicates to cloud storage or to the doctor for consultation. In between, the network can be breached by an attacker to gain access to personal and private data.

6. Expensive: Some wearables are very expensive and are not affordable to normal people. For example, Apple smartwatches, Armill smart jewelry, Google glass, etc.

7. Integration: Some wearables are not capable to work alone due to their very small size. They are integrated with some other device or technology. For example, a smartwatch needs to be integrated with a smartphone for most of the functionalities.

1.4 Research Work Done in the Healthcare Sector

A lot of research work has been done and some research work is still going on about these wearables to help in diagnosing various diseases. The main issue is regarding privacy and security. Privacy is a state of being alone or keeping someone's identity or information secret, whereas security is the state of feeling secure and free from anxiety, anger, fear, etc. means something that gives you assurance of being safe and secure.

Table 1.1 shows details of some modern smart wearables and the technology "discovered by various researchers and" used in them along with their advantages and limitations.

1.5 Advantages and Disadvantages

We have seen a lot of advantages of IoT in the healthcare sector including remote monitoring, remote doctor and medical facilities, making hospitals smart, etc. Reducing emergency room time; tracking patients, staff, and inventory; enhancing drug management; and ensuring the availability of critical smart devices are some of the major benefits of IoT healthcare [32,33]. The wearables are also adding effectiveness to the technology. But there are still some challenges that need to be worked upon.

1. Requires connectivity and lots of memory: If a person wants to take advantage of smart hospitals, he or she should be connected to the internet all the time. IoT sensors and devices require lots of memory to store the details of the patient and doctor and other important data.
2. Frequent and regular updates: As it is a combination of hardware and software, the details keep on adding and changing leading to various and frequent software updates. All the software must be updated timely to run accurately and stay as its latest version.
3. Security: The major concern of IoT devices is security. As the devices are interconnected with the help of the internet, there is a maximum chance of the data being attacked or hacked by unauthorized users or attackers. Cybercriminals can hack and misuse IoT device data for fraudulent health privileges or the formation of forged IDs for purchasing or vending medical drugs.
4. Privacy issues: IoT technology-based healthcare applications can be hacked or attacked easily by unauthorized hackers. For example, anyone with a fake identity can be a doctor

Table 1.1 Some Modern Smart Methodologies Developed for Disease Diagnosis

PAPER DETAIL	TECHNOLOGY USED AND DISCUSSED	ADVANTAGES OR BENEFICIAL FOR	LIMITATIONS & FUTURE WORK
A. Kumar et.al [18]	Blockchain with Industry4.0 and healthcare system healthcare4.0	Distributed and well-managed approach, automated, immutable, transparent, security, protection from data tampering, fault tolerance, QoS, data redundancy, etc.	In the future, the proposed work will be extended to be implemented over various Blockchain networks with different tools and techniques.
Kadhim et.al [19]	Internet-based Healthcare Monitor System (HCMS) with WSN security model	Secures collected data and monitor the health history of patients in the hospital.	Hospital management becomes very expensive.
Dwivedi et.al [20]	Proposed Embedded technology of IoT & Blockchain with remote health monitoring with some cryptographic primitives	It provided secure management and analysis of healthcare big data. It claims to diminish several attacks such as DoS, modification attacks, etc.	Resource constraints of IoT are key challenges and it was costlier also.
Swamy T. J et.al [21]	IoT system is offered and established with the help of oxygen saturation amount sensor, temperature sensor, BP sensor, Bluetooth, Arduino, and APP technologies.	The app generated by their proposed work is capable of having effective communication between doctor and patient. The accuracy and performance of the proposed work give satisfactory results.	In the future chatting feature will be incorporated. It can be extended with the support of wireless sensor technology, routing, placement & cognitive radio-established spectrum sensing.
Akkas et.al [22]	The authors covered the application of IoT technology in medicine. They proposed a system for collecting medical data using ZigBee.	Low power consumption and result came out was reliable, feasible, and self-configurable.	Specific to only very few factors monitoring
Sasubilli SM et.al [23]	IoT with Big data and for data storage they used Amazon cloud service in place of some local server.	They collected data from tribal people and focused on having less price and time-saving treatment. Other Advantages include availability, Flexibility, etc.	Existing work stores the data on cloud storage, and they will try to use fog computing for better optimization and more efficiency.
Obaidulla-Al-Mahmud et.al [24]	Proposed a smart IoT healthcare that consists of an intelligent medicine box.	It helps the patient to take the right medicine at right time along with the email.	Not secure as data is stored on a central server and then goes to the doctor for analysis.

(Continued)

Table 1.1 (Continued) Some Modern Smart Methodologies Developed for Disease Diagnosis

PAPER DETAIL	TECHNOLOGY USED AND DISCUSSED	ADVANTAGES OR BENEFICIAL FOR	LIMITATIONS & FUTURE WORK
Amaraweera et.al [25]	IoT technologies in the healthcare sector.	The author analyzed existing work regarding privacy and security in IoT Healthcare.	None
Maduri P.K. et.al [26]	Electronic-based technologies that measure physiological parameters	The kit is portable and affordable. It is based on Arduino which performs electrocardiography, electromyography, etc.	Only limited to sweet gland activity, BP, and body temperature. This will be acceptable in the future in disaster-prone areas.
Md. Raseduzzaman Ruman et.al [27]	They proposed a system that collects pulse, the temperature of the body (by LM35), and heart rate (by ECG) from a patient's body using a microcontroller, Arduino Mega, IoT cloud & WIFI module.	The author's main aim was to monitor patient health with a wireless body area network. The proposed system was user-friendly and cost-effective. It provides virtual consultation.	Not accurate because several sensors were used less and cost. It was very complex and difficult to analyze patients' health based on three parameters.
Ramani, J. Geetha, et.al [28]	Raspberry Pi coded with python, sensors were used to sense pulse, temperature, BP, and energy.	The proposed system helps the doctor to diagnose employees anytime anywhere with help of data collected from employees & transferred by using the internet	Can be further improvised by interfacing with more health parameter sensors.
E. N Ganesh [29]	Health monitoring system using Raspberry Pi, IoT, sensors, and LCD to display results.	The proposed system looks for heartbeat and body temperature and uses Wi-Fi to transfer the data on a phone or PC.	Large data repositories are required.
Sreekanth KU et.al [30]	They review concepts and existing technology in healthcare. They discussed the working of ubiquitous wearable devices.	The IoT-based healthcare system will be able to monitor heart rate, temperature sensor, blood pressure sensor, etc. and can predict the disease in advance	Expensive and not 100% accurate.
Khan et.al [31]	They proposed a complete monitoring existence cycle and effective healthcare monitoring system using IoT and RFID	The combination of microcontrollers with sensors has increased the power of IoT.	Costlier

online or the record of any patient can be hacked, changed, or breached by an attacker online.

5. Technical faults: As it is a technology made up of hardware and software, we cannot rely totally on it. It can be hacked, attacked by viruses, or can be malfunctioned. In that case, the life of the patient will be at greater risk.

6. Data overload and accuracy: Because of the non-uniformity of data and communication protocols, it is tough to summarize data for vital visions and analysis. The data is captured from time to time from the patient's body, which causes overloading of data. Also, this overloading can have an effect in taking the correct decision. IoT gathers data in bulk for proper analysis, which can cause overloading and that may lead to creating problems in getting an accurate result with correct precisions.

7. Cost: The IoT technology requires a lot of intake money in planning IoT applications for healthcare. So it would not be wrong if will conclude that IoT is expensive. Some examples are smart contact lenses, IoT-powered hearables, smartwatches, etc.

8. Multiple devices and protocol integration: The IoT works with the integration of sensors, devices, and protocols that can cause hindrance because of the different ecosystems used for every other IoT device's environment. This non-uniformity can cause reduction in the procedure and diminishes the choice of scalability of IoT in healthcare.

Apart from all these, the security issue is still the most challenging one in IoT technologies. Transferring data over a safe wireless network is still the most challenging one. The various key security requirements include:

- Data integrity i.e., the information of the patient should not be tampered with or altered by any attacker,
- Data confidentiality i.e., the medical history or medical sensed or recorded data should not be available to any third unauthorized person,
- Authentication i.e., the identity and authenticity of the patient and doctors is equally important to distinguish the fake doctors or patients,
- Non-repudiation i.e., a sensor node cannot deny after sending data to a doctor or at cloud remote storage.

1.6 Conclusion

Smart devices and wearables are offering novel and innovative opportunities in various areas, especially in the healthcare sector. This smart system first collects data from the patient's body with the help of sensors and then that vital health data is shared over a secure network. This data is then processed and diagnosed for further medications and prescriptions by the doctors. In this chapter, we have seen the emerging journey of IoT from basic to the most needed technology used almost everywhere, the components of IoT, the various application areas of IoT, the smart wearables, the variations of IoT such as HIoT, BIoT, SIoT, MioT, etc., IoT in the healthcare sector in which we have discussed smart hospitals, the process of healthcare IoT, and application of healthcare IoT. Apart from so many advantages of this technology, it suffers from some challenges and problems. The challenges faced by smart devices include power problems, storage problems, security, and privacy issues. A lot of research work is going on to get a healthier and easier life with the combination of IoT technology and telemedicine. In the future, IoT will help in creating more smart hospitals and will also help in creating more customized and patient-oriented technology that will enable the patient more accurate and safe personalized care without visiting hospitals.

References

[1] *IoT Security: Advances in Authentication*, First Edition. Edited by Madhusanka Liyanage, An Braeken, Pardeep Kumar, and Mika Ylianttila. 2020 John Wiley & Sons Ltd. Published 2020 by John Wiley & Sons Ltd.

[2] [online] https://ordr.net/article/iot-healthcare-examples/

[3] https://www.embeddedcomputing.com/application/healthcare/telehealth-healthcare-iot/how-iot-is-transforming-the-healthcare-industry

[4] Dian, F. John, Reza Vahidnia, and Alireza Rahmati. "Wearables and the Internet of Things (IoT), applications, opportunities, and challenges: A Survey." *IEEE Access* 8 (2020): 69200–69211.

[5] [online] https://www.iberdrola.com/innovation/home-automation

[6] [online] https://www.twi-global.com/technical-knowledge/faqs/what-is-a-smart-city.

[7] [online] https://smartenergyusa.com/what-is-smart-energy/

[8] Ben Fekih, Rim, and Mariam Lahami. "Application of Blockchain Technology in Healthcare: A Comprehensive Study." International

Conference on Smart Homes and Health Telematics. Springer, Cham, 2020.

[9] Karunarathne, Sivanarayani M., Neetesh Saxena, and Muhammad Khurram Khan. "Security and privacy in IoT smart healthcare." *IEEE Internet Computing* 25.4 (2021): 37–48.

[10] Dian, F. John, Reza Vahidnia, and Alireza Rahmati. "Wearables and the Internet of Things (IoT), applications, opportunities, and challenges: A Survey." *IEEE Access* 8 (2020): 69200–69211.

[11] Vishnu, S., SR Jino Ramson, and R. Jegan. "Internet of Medical Things (IoMT)-An Overview." 2020 5th International Conference on Devices, Circuits and Systems (ICDCS). IEEE, 2020.

[12] Takiddeen, Nour, and Imran Zualkernan. "Smartwatches as IoT Edge Devices: A Framework and Survey." 2019 Fourth International Conference on Fog and Mobile Edge Computing (FMEC). IEEE, 2019.

[13] Reeder, Blaine, and Alexandria David. "Health at hand: A systematic review of smart watch uses for health and wellness." *Journal of Biomedical Informatics* 63 (2016): 269–276.

[14] Park, Jihun, et al. "Soft, smart contact lenses with integrations of wireless circuits, glucose sensors, and displays." *Science Advances* 4.1 (2018): eaap9841.

[15] Patel, Jayun, and Ragib Hasan. "Smart Bracelets: Towards Automating Personal Safety using Wearable Smart Jewelry." 2018 15th IEEE Annual Consumer Communications & Networking Conference (CCNC). IEEE, 2018.

[16] Qiu, Hao, Xianping Wang, and Fei Xie. "A Survey on Smart Wearables in the Application of Fitness." 2017 IEEE 15th Intl Conf on Dependable, Autonomic and Secure Computing, 15th Intl Conf on Pervasive Intelligence and Computing, 3rd Intl Conf on Big Data Intelligence and Computing and Cyber Science and Technology Congress (DASC/PiCom/DataCom/CyberSciTech). IEEE, 2017.

[17] Wu, Taiyang, et al. "An autonomous wireless body area network implementation towards IoT connected healthcare applications." *IEEE Access* 5 (2017): 11413–11422.

[18] Vo, Anh Tuan, and Hee-Jun Kang. "A novel fault-tolerant control method for robot manipulators based on non-singular fast terminal sliding mode control and disturbance observer." *IEEE Access* 8 (2020): 109388–109400.

[19] Kadhim, Kadhim Takleef, et al. "An overview of patient's health status monitoring system based on Internet of Things (IoT)." *Wireless Personal Communications* 114.3 (2020): 2235–2262.

[20] Dwivedi, Ashutosh Dhar, et al. "A decentralized privacy-preserving healthcare blockchain for IoT." *Sensors* 19.2 (2019): 326.

[21] Swamy, T. Jagannadha, and T. N. Murthy. "Esmart: An IoT Based Intelligent Health Monitoring and Management System for Mankind." 2019 International Conference on Computer Communication and Informatics (ICCCI). IEEE, 2019.

[22] Akkaş, M. Alper, Radosveta Sokullu, and H. Ertürk Çetin. "Healthcare and patient monitoring using IoT." *Internet of Things* 11 (2020): 100173.

[23] Sasubilli, Satya Murthy, Abhishek Kumar, and Vishal Dutt. "Improving Health Care by Help of Internet of Things and Bigdata Analytics and Cloud Computing." 2020 International Conference on Advances in Computing and Communication Engineering (ICACCE). IEEE, 2020.

[24] Al-Mahmud, Obaidulla, et al. "Internet of Things (IoT) Based Smart Health Care Medical Box for Elderly People." 2020 International Conference for Emerging Technology (INCET). IEEE, 2020.

[25] Amaraweera, Suvini P., and Malka N. Halgamuge. "Internet of Things in the Healthcare Sector: Overview of Security and Privacy Issues." *Security, privacy and trust in the IoT environment* (2019): 153–179.

[26] Maduri, Praveen Kumar, et al. "IOT Based Patient Health Monitoring Portable Kit." 2020 2nd International Conference on Advances in Computing, Communication Control and Networking (ICACCCN). IEEE, 2020.

[27] Ruman, Md Raseduzzaman, et al. "IoT Based Emergency Health Monitoring System." 2020 International Conference on Industry 4.0 Technology (I4Tech). IEEE, 2020.

[28] Ramani, J. Geetha, et al. "IOT Based Employee Health Monitoring System." 2020 6th International Conference on Advanced Computing and Communication Systems (ICACCS). IEEE, 2020.

[29] Ganesh, E. N. "Implementation of digital notice board using raspberry pi and iot." *Oriental Journal of Computer Science and Technology* 12.1 (2019): 14–20.

[30] Sreekanth, K. U., and K. P. Nitha. "A study on health care in Internet of Things." *International Journal on Recent and Innovation Trends in Computing and Communication* 4.2 (2016): 44–47.

[31] Khan, Sarfraz Fayaz "Health care monitoring system in Internet of Things (IoT) by using RFID", In 2017 6th International Conference on Industrial Technology and Management (ICITM), pages 198–204, 2017.

[32] Sapra, V., M. L. Saini, and L. Verma. "Identification of Coronary Artery Disease using Artificial Neural Network and Case-Based Reasoning." *Recent Advances in Computer Science and Communications (Formerly: Recent Patents on Computer Science)* 14 (8) (2021): 2651–2661.

[33] Sapra, V., and L. Sapra. "Early Detection of Type 2 Diabetes Mellitus Using Deep Neural Network–Based Model." *Advanced Healthcare Systems: Empowering Physicians with IoT-Enabled Technologies* (2022): 305–317.

2

Secure Blockchain-Based Intelligent Internet of Things

SIMA DAS[1], NIMAY CHANDRA GIRI[2],
KAUSHIK MAZUMDAR[3],
PARIJAT BHOWMICK[4],
HIMANSHU TIWARI[5], DIVYA PANT[6], AND
SHILPA MEHTA[7]

[1]Department of Computer Science
and Engineering, Bengal College of
Engineering and Technology,
Durgapur, West Bengal, India
[2]Department of Electronics and
Communication Engineering and
Centre for Renewable Energy and
Environment, Centurion University
of Technology and Management,
Odisha, India
[3]Department of Electronics and
Communication Engineering, IIT
Dhanbad (ISM) India
[4]Department of Electrical and
Electronics and Communication
Engineering, IIT Guwahati, Assam,
India
[5]Department of Agronomy, Sardar
Vallabhbhai Patel University of
Agriculture and Technology, Meerut,
India
[6]Plant Science Department,
Pennsylvania State University,
University Park, State College,
Pennsylvania, U.S.A.
[7]Department of Electrical and
Electronic Engineering, Auckland
University of Technology,
New Zealand

DOI: 10.1201/9781003269168-2

23

Abstract

Online security is the performance of safe platforms, administrations, and developments of electronic system attacks. The cyberattacks are characteristically pointed in the direction of accomplishment to, varying, or defeating delicate facts; blackmailing for cash from customers; or interfering in regular commercial actions. Carrying out viable system protection actions is the most difficult task today as there are a huge number of devices compared to people, and attackers are turning out to be more imaginative. Through the progression of data and communication origination, also extension of sensor advancements, the Internet of Things is nowadays being largely applied in smart homes for effective strength management and inescapable detecting. In smart households, different IoT devices are accompanied by other devices, and these links are fixed on doors. The living of ways in smart homes is critical; in all circumstances, its unified design presents different security weaknesses like uprightness, confirmation, and accessibility. The organization comprises three layers including gadget, gateway, and cloud layers. Blockchain modernization is applied at the front entrance in which information is placed away and operated in the construction of blockchain to support decentralization besides overthrowing the problem as a predictable intense proposal. The blockchain assures the morality of data confidentiality and exterior of the smart system also gives accessibility over authentication and accomplished communication among systems. In this chapter, we propose architecture for secure blockchain-based intelligent Internet of Things and also discuss application area, advantages, and limitations of the proposed work.

2.1 Introduction

The blockchain is a distributed database of statistics of all transactions or digital occasions that have been carried out and shared amongst parties [1–3]. Consistent with an international marketplace survey by the company Gartner, the wide variety of smart domestic gadgets is predicted to produce 25 billion units through 2020. The growing rate of the worldwide smart home marketplace is predicted to increase by $7 billion by 2025 [4,5]. With the growing complexity of network topologies and architectures, adding intelligence to the community managed plane through artificial intelligence and machine learning (AI&ML) is turning into a trend in system development [6–8]. In addition to these, AI/ML techniques are being attempted or postulated in nearly all steps of network lifecycle management, such as issue and sub-system improvement, network orchestration, facet aid management, and community slice control [9]. The deficiency of intrinsic safety technology in the modern-day Internet of Things (IoT) systems brings forth numerous protection vulnerabilities and privacy risks [10].

The rest of the sections are as follows: Survey on blockchain-based smart secure system is discussed in section 2.2; proposed work for secure blockchain-based intelligent Internet of Things will be discussed in section 2.3; advantages and limitations of secure blockchain-based intelligent Internet of Things will be discussed in section 2.4; and a summary of the chapter will be concluded in section 2.5.

2.2 Literature Survey

In this section, a literature survey will be discussed.

Internet of Things (IoT) is combining the latest technology together with the blockchain toward beautifying system safety. Though, the blockchain expresses several barriers, inclusive of aid needs, electricity necessities, scalability, and high latency. The paper affords an innovative blockchain shape that connects with a multi-blockchain in a single ledger with the usage of a directed acyclic graph (DAG) structure known as a multi-chain. The multi-chain shape determines the problems of scalability and is an applicant to replace the conventional blockchain with a cyber system. This paper as well introduces an innovative system known as "Multi-Chain Proof of Rapid Authentication" (McPoRA) to enhance latency, which remains the critical element in IoT aid-restricted gadgets. McPoRA is around 4000X quicker than proof-of-work (PoW), and 55X quicker than proof-of-authentication (PoAh) [11].

A blockchain is the gathering of the blocks together with digital property, these blocks through digital statistics join as a sequence over a node with a record. The chapter gives a summary of blockchain in addition to its key phrases; besides blockchain-constructed programs in special regions. It consists of what method blockchain facilitates inside the healthcare enterprise, saving healthcare scams, storing and dealing with electronic health records (EHRs), Industry 4.0 systems with blockchain, blockchain inside the internet, and blockchain-based cyber-physical system [12].

In this era, we are witnessing the rapid development of emerging technologies, and it is remarkable how blockchain is being used to distinguish modern discoveries. The article examines a number of security issues that can be addressed through blockchain technology. It thoroughly analyzes each problem, aiming to identify key challenges faced by existing data sharing platforms that rely on trusted third parties, as well as security concerns associated with them. The article also explores how blockchain and data technology advancements can address these problems. Additionally, it aims to present the advantages and disadvantages of using blockchain for information security in various sectors of companies. By doing so, it contributes to the enhancement of cybersecurity systems, which are highly relevant to these sectors in terms of securing data processing strategies and facilitating intelligent decision-making in real-world applications. The method employed involves applying data security measures, leveraging knowledge of system acquisition methods to assess cyber risks, and ultimately seeking to improve cybersecurity measures [13].

Recently, system-on-chip (SoC) strategies encompass a huge kind of incredibly touchy property that ought to be protected from unauthorized entry. A substantial element of SoC design includes the study, evaluation, and assessment of resiliency strategies toward attacks on some property. These attacks might also increase since the number of assets, which includes malicious blocks inside the computer hardware, malicious and otherwise inclined firmware and software, the uncertain conversation of the device by different gadgets, and channel vulnerabilities via authority and performance. Security actions for these attacks are similarly varied, encompassing architecture, layout, implementation, and validation-based total protection. In this paper, we offer an inclusive review of the safety structure in current SoC proposals, together with resiliency strategies and their validation models at pre-silicon and post-silicon phases. They discover breaks in evaluation architectures, advance strategy, and validation to report. To conclude, they offer industry views proceeding the function and effect of cutting-edge performance on SoC safety and also speak of a few rising traits in this critical place [14].

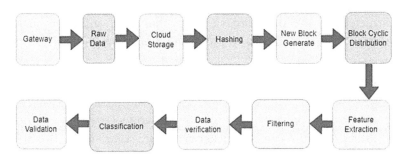

Figure 2.1   Proposed architecture for secure blockchain-based intelligent internet of things.

2.3 Proposed Work

In this section, we will discuss the proposed method for the chapter. The proposed work, as shown in Figure 2.1, is executed in a step-by-step procedure. The steps are as follows: gateway, raw data collection, cloud storage, hashing, new block generation, block-cyclic distribution, feature extraction, filtering, data verification, classification, and the last step is data validation.

2.3.1 Gateway

The gateway is implemented with a secure hash, a cryptographic algorithm that is used to encrypt the gateway statistics to the system and start communication.

2.3.2 Raw Data Collection

The gateway creates a request message and sends it to the device for dataset acquisition from the device.

2.3.3 Cloud Storage

The gateway receives raw data by deciphering it and stores it in a cloud platform.

2.3.4 Hashing

Using the secure hash algorithm (SHA), the sensitive information of smart homes can be secure. The SHA algorithm is implemented and constructed on the password stated by the user, and then shared information is protected by the hash function.

2.3.5 New Block Generate

The system can generate new blocks and connect with the blockchain; the procedure can be quicker and more secure using the SHA technique.

2.3.6 Distribution

Blockchain facilitates the distribution of the fee of running a platform with various members by equally measuring and rewards. The decentralized model is used for blockchain and cloud-based security systems.

2.3.7 Feature Extraction

The fundamental concept of the feature method is a very simple and effective method. In applying ICA to feature selection, we encompass output class records similarly to input features. In this proposed work, selected features are as follows: gateway ID, hardware information, software information, and connected device information.

2.3.8 Filtering

For better performance in the cloud space, it filters and reserves information required with the aid of the router, based totally on machine identity and then it is kept with the standardization and category technique.

2.3.9 Data Verification

Data is exchanged and configured using blockchain. Information is interchanged in a verifiable way between unknown people that are linked with a node-to-node community.

2.3.10 Classification

The proposed system classifies information coming into the gateway and therefore desired facts may be hashed, encrypted, and stored inside the cloud record using a back propagation neural network (BPNN).

2.3.11 Data Validation

After classification using BPNN, the security investigation is accomplished to authenticate the act of our proposed architecture.

2.4 Advantages and Limitations of Secure Blockchain-Based IIoT

The advantages and limitations of secure blockchain are based on the intelligence of Internet of Things and will be discussed in this section.

2.4.1 Advantages of Blockchain–Based Security

The blockchain has several application areas, including healthcare [15] and the cybersecurity domain [16]. The advantages of blockchain-based Internet of Things (as shown in Figure 2.2) are as follows.

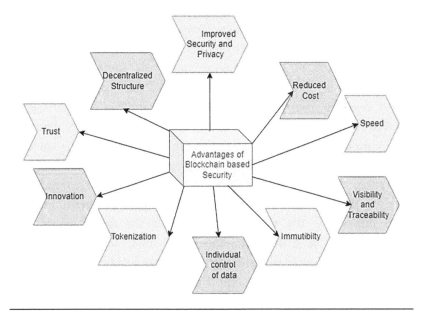

Figure 2.2   Advantages of blockchain-based security.

2.4.1.1 Trust   Blockchain facilitates consensus among unique entities, even in cases where consensus is imaginary or unproven. Consequently, these entities are more inclined to engage in business connections involving data distribution or connections that would not have been possible otherwise or would have required significant intermediaries. The most widely recognized advantage of blockchain technology is its ability to foster trust. This value is evident in early use cases of blockchain, where it enabled communication between entities that lacked direct associations but still needed to share information or settle transactions. Bitcoin and other cryptocurrencies serve as prime examples of how blockchain enables consensus among individuals who have no prior knowledge of each other.

2.4.1.2 Decentralized Structure   Blockchain demonstrates its value particularly in situations where there is no central authority to establish trust, according to Daniel Field, the founder of Blockchain, a global provider of digital technology and services. Therefore, in addition to enabling trust among participants who are unfamiliar with each other, blockchain allows for the sharing of data within organizational environments where no single entity has complete control. A supply chain is a perfect example: various suppliers, transportation companies, manufacturers, distributors, and retailers all require information from others in the chain, but there is no single entity responsible for facilitating comprehensive data distribution. Blockchain, through its decentralized nature, resolves this predicament.

2.4.1.3 Improved Security and Privacy   The protection of blockchain-aided structures is another main advantage of this evolving generation. The boosted safety supplied by blockchain branches from in what way the expertise essentially the whole thing: Blockchain generates an irreversible document of communications through end-to-end encryption that closes scams and illegal movement. Furthermore, statistics proceeding the blockchain are saved throughout a web of computer systems, making it almost unbearable to hack (not like conservative computer systems that keep facts organized in servers). Additionally, blockchain can report privacy issues better than traditional computer structures by means of anonymizing facts and needing approvals to get right of entry.

2.4.1.4 Reduced Costs Blockchain can cut charges for officialdoms. It produces products in transaction processing. The aforementioned additionally decreases guide responsibilities like accumulating and modifying records and also eases reporting and auditing procedures. Specialists mark on the economic investments that monetarists understand once the practice of blockchain, explanation that blockchain's competence to update clearance and arrangement interprets at once into a technique to save amount.

2.4.1.5 Speed By getting rid of intermediaries, in addition to changing last-guide techniques in communications, blockchain can switch connections quicker than conservative strategies. In many instances, blockchain can grip an operation in seconds or less. Nevertheless, epochs container range; in what way a blockchain-primarily based gadget can method transactions depend on multiple factors, along with by what method each block of facts is and web traffic. Specialists have determined that blockchain generally strokes many strategies and skills in phrases of rapidity.

2.4.1.6 Visibility and Traceability Walmart's custom of blockchain is just not around speed; the capacity to trace the foundation of merchandise. This permits stores like Walmart to recover, manipulate records, respond to troubles or inquiries and affirm the pasts of its merchandise. According to professionals, blockchain can assist to track the roots of a ramification of objects, along with remedies to authorize they may be authentic rather than fake and natural gadgets to authorize they are certainly organic.

2.4.1.7 Immutability Immutableness truly means that communications, after being recorded at the blockchain, cannot be transformed or otherwise removed. In the blockchain, entire transactions are time-stamped and date-stamped; there is an everlasting document. Blockchain can be used to tune records over the years, permitting a comfortable, reliable audit of statistics.

2.4.1.8 Individual Control of Data Blockchain allows an exceptional quantity of character regulator concluded individual digital facts, professionals. "In a world in which facts are a very treasured commodity, the generation inherently protects the facts that belong to you whilst permitting you to govern it".

2.4.1.9 Tokenization   Tokenization is the method in which the cost of a strength (whether real or virtual) is transformed by a virtual token and is verified after which it is shared through blockchain. Tokenization has been trapped through digital art and different digital assets; however, tokenization takes broader packages that could smooth enterprise transactions.

2.4.1.10 Innovation   Privileged transversely more than one industry is reconnoitering and enforcing blockchain-based structures on the way to clear up inflexible issues and progress with venerable substantial performance. Studies have continuously shown that a strong percentage of people falsify their resumes, leaving hiring managers with the time-consuming project of manually verifying the records.

2.4.2 Limitation of Blockchain-Based Security

Limitations of the blockchain-based Internet of Things (as shown in Figure 2.3) are as follows.

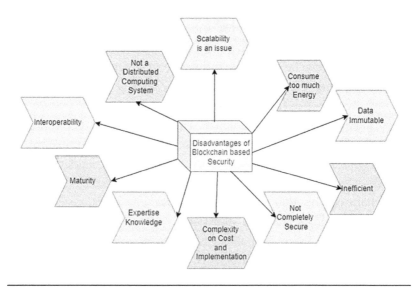

Figure 2.3   Disadvantages of blockchain-based security.

2.4.2.1 Blockchain Is Not a Distributed Computing System Blockchain is a community that relies on nodes to characterize properly. The niceness of the nodes determines the first-rate of the blockchain.

2.4.2.2 Scalability Is an Issue Blockchains aren't as scalable as their counterpart centralized machines. If you have used the Bitcoin network, then you would understand that the transactions are completed depending on the community congestion. This hassle is associated with scalability troubles with blockchain networks.

2.4.2.3 Some Blockchain Solutions Consume Too Much Energy The blockchain era was added with Bitcoin. It makes use of the proof-of-work consensus set of rules that relied on the miners to do the hard work. The miners are incentivized to remedy complicated mathematical problems. The high power intake is what makes those complicated mathematical problems no longer so perfect for the actual global.

2.4.2.4 Data Immutable Data immutability has constantly been one of the biggest hazards of the blockchain. It is clear that multiple systems have advantages from it that include delivery chains, monetary structures, and so forth. However, if you take how networks paint, you must understand that this immutability can only be present if the community nodes are disbursed pretty.

2.4.2.5 Blockchains Are Sometimes Inefficient Right now, there are a couple of blockchain technologies out there. If you select the maximum popular ones together with the blockchain technology used by Bitcoin, you may discover plenty of inefficiencies within the system. This is one of the huge dangers of blockchain.

2.4.2.6 Not Completely Secure The blockchain era is more at ease than other systems. However, this doesn't suggest that it isn't always completely comfy.

2.4.2.7 Complexity on Cost and Implementation The underlying value of implementing blockchain generation is huge. Even though most of the blockchain solutions together with hyperledger are open source, they require quite a lot of funding from the agency that is willing to pursue it. There are expenses associated with hiring developers, managing a team that excels at special elements of the blockchain era, licensing expenses if you choose a paid blockchain answer, and so on.

2.4.2.8 Expertise Knowledge Implementing and dealing with a blockchain project is difficult. It calls for thorough information from the enterprise to go through the complete procedure. They want to hire more than one professional within the blockchain field, which leads to a problem and as a result, it is counted as one of the dangers of blockchain.

2.4.2.9 Maturity Blockchain generation is only a decade antique. This approach is a new era that calls for time to mature. If you take the specific consortium into consideration, you may note multiple players looking to remedy the decentralized hassle with their particular answer.

2.4.2.10 Interoperability The interoperability trouble also persists while it comes to conventional structures and systems using blockchain technology.

2.5 Conclusion

The chapter is designed for blockchain-based gateway architecture. The proposed method offers a secure platform for the heterogeneous Internet of Things. The proposed system accommodates machine gateway, cloud layers, and blockchain. Blockchain is applied on the front entrance in which records are placed away and operated within the construction of blockchain to help decentralization, besides overthrowing the limitation as a predictable excessive concept. The blockchain assures the morality of the statistics confidentiality and exterior of the clever domestic system and also offers accessibility over authentication and finished conversation among structures. In this chapter, we proposed system architecture for a secure blockchain-based intelligent Internet of Things, and also discussed the application of the proposed system in different fields; last but not least, we also discussed advantages and limitations of the proposed system.

References

1. X. Yang, Y. Chen and X. Chen, "Effective Scheme against 51% Attack on Proof-of-Work Blockchain with History Weighted Information," *2019 IEEE International Conference on Blockchain (Blockchain)*, 2019, pp. 261–265, doi: 10.1109/Blockchain.2019.00041.
2. S. Das, J. Das, S. Modak and K. Mazumdar. (2022). "Internet of Things with Machine Learning based smart Cardiovascular disease classifier for Healthcare in Secure platform".
3. S. Malik, V. Dedeoglu, S. S. Kanhere and R. Jurdak, "TrustChain: Trust Management in Blockchain and IoT Supported Supply Chains," *2019 IEEE International Conference on Blockchain (Blockchain)*, 2019, pp. 184–193, doi: 10.1109/Blockchain.2019.00032.
4. R. J. Robles, T. H. Kim, D. Cook and S. Das. (2010). "A Review on Security in Smart Home Development." *Int J Adv Sci Technol.* 15, 13–22.
5. Y. Lee, S. Rathore, J. H. Park et al. (2020). "A Blockchain-Based Smart Home Gateway Architecture for Preventing Data Forgery." *Hum. Cent. Comput. Inf. Sci.* 10, 9. 10.1186/s13673-020-0214-5.
6. H. Yao, T. Mai, C. Jiang, L. Kuang and S. Guo. (Nov. 2019). "AI Routers & Network Mind: A Hybrid Machine Learning Paradigm for Packet Routing." in *IEEE Computational Intelligence Magazine* 14 (4), 21–30, doi: 10.1109/MCI.2019.2937609.
7. S. Das, L. Ghosh and S. Saha, (2020). "Analyzing Gaming Effects on Cognitive Load Using Artificial Intelligent Tools." 10.1109/CONECCT50063.2020.9198662.
8. S. Das and A. Bhattacharya. (2021). "ECG Assess Heartbeat rate, Classifying using BPNN while Watching Movie and send Movie Rating through Telegram." 465–474. 10.1007/978-981-15-9774-9_43.
9. B. Raghothaman. (December 2021). "Training, Testing and Validation Challenges for Next Generation AI/ML-Based Intelligent Wireless Networks." in *IEEE Wireless Communications* 28 (6), 5–6. doi: 10.1109/MWC.2021.9690485.
10. S. Saxena, B. Bhushan and M. Ahad. (2021). "Blockchain based solutions to secure IoT: Background, Integration Trends and a Way Forward." *Journal of Network and Computer Applications.* 181, 103050. 10.1016/j.jnca.2021.103050.
11. A. Alkhodair, S. Mohanty, E. Kougianos and D. Puthal, "McPoRA: A Multi-chain Proof of Rapid Authentication for Post-Blockchain Based Security in Large Scale Complex Cyber-Physical Systems," *2020 IEEE Computer Society Annual Symposium on VLSI (ISVLSI)*, 2020, pp. 446–451, doi: 10.1109/ISVLSI49217.2020.00-16.
12. S. M. Tadaka and L. Tawalbeh, "Applications of Blockchain in Healthcare, Industry 4, and Cyber-Physical Systems," *2020 7th International Conference on Internet of Things: Systems, Management and*

Security (IOTSMS), 2020, pp. 1–8, doi: 10.1109/IOTSMS52051.2020. 9340215.

13. P. Grover and S. Prasad, "A Review on Block chain and Data Mining Based Data Security Methods," *2021 2nd International Conference on Big Data Analytics and Practices (IBDAP)*, 2021, pp. 112–118, doi: 10.1109/IBDAP52511.2021.9552120.

14. S. Ray, E. Peeters, M. M. Tehranipoor and S. Bhunia, "System-on-Chip Platform Security Assurance: Architecture and Validation," in *Proceedings of the IEEE*, vol. 106, no. 1, pp. 21–37, Jan. 2018, doi: 10.1109/JPROC.2017.2714641.

15. S. Das, J. Das, S. Modak and K. Mazumdar (2022). "Internet of Things with Machine Learning based smart Cardiovascular disease classifier for Healthcare in Secure platform".

16. S. Das, A. K. Balmiki and K. Mazumdar (2022). "The Role of AI-ML Techniques in Cyber Security". 10.4018/978-1-6684-3991-3.

3

AN INTELLECTUAL ANALYSIS OF STRUCTURAL HEALTHCARE SYSTEMS IN INDIA USING INTELLIGENCE-BASED TECHNIQUES

NAFEES AKHTER FAROOQUI[1], RITIKA MEHRA[2], AND SAMRAH BUTOOL FARIDI[3]

[1]BBD University, Lucknow, India
[2]Dev Bhoomi Uttarakhand University, Dehradun, India
[3]Era University, Lucknow, India

Abstract

Human beings are known to be Mother Earth's intelligent creatures and are naturally more health conscious. Humanity has developed numerous established healthcare systems since the ages. Healthcare systems and policies play a critical role in deciding how health services are provided, used, and affect health outcomes. India has a comprehensive healthcare system, but there are still many qualitative differences between rural and urban areas as well as between public and private healthcare. With the increase of urbanization in India, the lifestyle of people has changed. Most lifestyle disease increases cholesterol, obesity, high blood pressure, poor diet, work pressure, and alcohol, which can be said that the current scenario of healthcare in India is in the worst condition. In our country, the doctor-patient ratio is continuously decreasing, and people are devoting themselves to their regular health check-ups. Therefore, machine learning techniques change the face of the healthcare system. Machine learning approaches are gaining popularity in the research

DOI: 10.1201/9781003269168-3

community to simplify the method and predict diseases perfectly. Machine learning approaches promote the creation of knowledge into a machine so that the learned experience can allow it to work better in the future. Application of machine learning methods on electronic health records could provide useful knowledge on health risk prediction. To new start-ups and major ICT companies offering intelligence solutions to the country's healthcare problems, the use of artificial intelligence techniques in healthcare in India is growing. Reducing the imbalanced proportion of qualified doctors to patients and making doctors more efficient, administering specialized care to remote regions, and retraining doctors and nurses in difficult therapies are challenges and alternatives. This chapter briefly explains the Indian public healthcare system and tracks the previous health programs and plans with a machine-learning technique that focuses on poor health resources in India.

3.1 Introduction

"Health is a state of complete physical, mental, and social well-being and not merely an absence of disease or infirmity."

Every individual's right to health is a fundamental human right, as well as a global societal aim. As a result, health might be defined as the ability to live a productive social and economic life. To achieve this, World Health Assembly in 1977 decided that the main aim in the next decade for governments should focus on how people can live economically fruitful life also termed health for all by 2000, decided at the Alma Ata conference. "Primary healthcare" is essential healthcare made commonly available to everyone and acceptable at low cost to the lower-income community for better health.

India was mostly a rural, agrarian economy. Around 1.25 billion people still reside in rural areas. India's booming economy, on the other hand, has average income rates, which is driving fast urbanization, producing a burgeoning middle class, and raising health insurance knowledge. In India, healthcare is one of the most important service industries. In India, the healthcare industry can be viewed as either half-empty or half-full. The industry faces numerous issues, including the need to reduce mortality rates, create physical infrastructure, offer health insurance, and assure the availability of educated medical personnel, among others. According to India's constitution, health is a state topic. Each state is responsible for making efforts to improve the health and living standards of the targeted population, as well as promoting public health as a primary function. Access to healthcare is determined by how healthcare is delivered.

The healthcare sector in India has improved dramatically during the previous few decades. The huge increase in health indicators, such as newborn mortality, maternal mortality, and birth life expectancy, among others, demonstrates this. Despite all these advantages in the healthcare sector, still India has a long way to go. The healthcare system is exceptional in every country, depending on its requirements and resources, but primary healthcare is the most universal component. To provide good healthcare services, certain countries' healthcare systems are divided among government agencies, private agencies, philanthropic groups, and religious organizations. Private hospitals, health professionals, medical colleges, program administrators, and so on are all part of the Indian healthcare system.

The healthcare system is made up of all acts and people whose major goal is to deliver high-quality healthcare and improve people's health. Health workers, hospitals, and healthcare agents have risen at a breakneck pace throughout this century. These agents have aided in the improvement of health, especially among the poor. As a result, an evaluation of India's current healthcare system is required. Any healthcare system would be incomplete without a good service delivery system. As a result, good healthcare delivery is critical and serves as a fundamental input into the population's health state. According to NFHS-3, about 70% of urban households and 63% of rural households use the private healthcare system as their major source of care. Despite government efforts, about 44% of all children are malnourished and maternal and child death rates are much higher. People rely on private-sector healthcare services more than public-sector providers for a variety of reasons, one of which is the public healthcare system's poor quality of care. The distance between primary health centers (PHCs), community health centers (CHCs), and sub-centers is the cause of the public health care system's low quality of care (SCs).

The Indian healthcare system has failed Indians on a variety of levels, particularly in rural areas. While the Indian healthcare system has or has access to the best technology and physicians, it nevertheless suffers from a lack of infrastructure in terms of primary healthcare, community health centers, and specialty centers. Because of India's federalized government system, the country's governance and health-care operations are split between the federal and state governments. Various programs for the health and welfare of families have been initiated by the Union's Ministry of Health and Family Welfare. Programs for the prevention of major communicable diseases, their prevention and promotion of advanced and original medicinal systems, and the establishment of standards and plans have also been initiated. In addition, the ministry supports states in preventing and controlling the spread of seasonal disease outbreaks and epidemics by providing technical assistance [1]. Public safety, healthcare, sanitation, and other areas, on the other hand, are under state control, making health a state duty. Furthermore, areas with national developments, such as birth control, family welfare, medical education, food adulteration preven-tion, and quality management in medicine production, are regulated jointly by the federal and state governments.

Artificial intelligence and machine learning have infiltrated prac-tically all real-world applications, resulting in a ubiquitous automated environment. Artificial intelligence has improved patient care and cut mortality rates in the medical industry. Precision robots that employ powerful AI technology to treat locations have improved diagnosis and therapy for some specific conditions such as cancer, vision dif-ficulties, and tumors. It has also created virtual doctors and medical robots, lowering the number of trips to hospitals by the old and disabled. Most robots are capable of doing minor procedures. However, such robots aren't intelligently created and can't be intel-ligent enough without artificial intelligence software that directs them to accomplish the activities listed above. Recent scientific developments in neural networking, natural language processing, image recognition software, and speech recognition have all helped to increase the performance of these robots.

In India, new start-ups and established ICT corporations are of-fering AI solutions to the country's healthcare concerns, indicating that the usage of AI in healthcare is growing. Resolving the unequal relationship between professional physicians and patients, as well as making physicians more effective at their professions, are some of the issues and solutions.

The supply of individualized services and superior-quality treatment to remote areas, as well as the training of doctors and nurses in sophisticated operations [2]. Unlike previous technologies that just enhanced human abilities, health AI now has the potential to considerably broaden the spectrum of human activity. Natural language processing, smart agents, computer vision, machine learning, expert systems, chatbots, and voice recognition are some of the other breakthroughs [3–6]. These techniques could be used to provide accurate results for a physician. At various levels, AI is being used and developed across the healthcare sector. Machine learning can be used to focus on heterogeneous "electronic health records" (EHRs) and these records are used to analyze for predictive modeling.

Machine learning is one of the fastest-rising disciplines in computer science and one of the major difficulties in health informatics. Electronic health records (EHRs) contain information about a huge number of individuals. The difficulty with large amounts of data is determining how the data should be analyzed and intelligence deduced. This is also known as "Rapid Learning Health Care (RLHC)", and it involves analyzing a big amount of data that is always increasing in order to anticipate accurate health risk and disease prediction models. Predictive modeling with EHRs is hampered by the difficulties of representing and analyzing patient data to create useful insights. Recent improvements in machine learning algorithm design and implementation on the EHR dataset have yielded promising results. Machine learning models that are state-of-the-art can help solve clinical problems that are difficult to solve using traditional methods [7,8].

The IoT is a system that connects different components and allows them to communicate over a network [9]. We can obtain the information with the help of sensors. This information gets from the computer networks which help in the proposed healthcare system. It allows hardware components to connect to the internet and create a system based on different advanced tools such as "Near Field Communication (NFC)" and "Wireless Sensor Networks (WSN)". The sensor provides data to the base station in a sensor network.

Smart bins, modern IoT-enabled irrigation systems and environmental monitoring, intelligent healthcare systems, and IoT-enabled traffic monitoring systems are some of the major application areas of IoT techniques. IoT enables different healthcare nursing devices to the healthcare infrastructure [10]. Healthcare is a system that focuses on improving people's health [11]. It has been observed in the last decade that lung- and heart-related illnesses are a major concern. Wireless technology like portable remote health monitoring devices and expert systems is a novel idea, which enables healthcare remote monitoring. In all cases, the Internet of Things (IoT) aids in disease detection and patient therapy [12,13].

Telemedicine is utilized to deal with health difficulties in developing nations such as India. When a clinician and a patient are not physically present, telemedicine is a technique of caring for them remotely. "The remote delivery of healthcare services" is defined as Telehealth Care System. Telemedicine provides several advantages, but it also has significant drawbacks. Providers, payers, and legislators all recognized that some gray zones are difficult to navigate. Over the next decade, the medical sector will grow very quickly but the operational face and technological challenges will impact the services.

This chapter suggests an advanced healthcare system that makes use of cutting-edge tools like the Internet of Things and machine learning. It is cheaper for people living in distant places; they can use it for better results. The chapter discusses contemporary break-throughs and research in the field of machine learning, as well as how to apply it to healthcare.

3.2 Healthcare System Structure of India

3.2.1 Health System

Health management is a division of community management that deals with materials involving the advancement of healthcare, prevention of disease, and development of infrastructure and manpower with medical education and training which aims to improve the physical, mental, and social well-being of people. Various health benefits are designed to meet the above-stated goals with the use of learning and sources through a well-designed health system as per the health needs, availability of resources, and vision of healthcare.

3.2.2 Themes of Health Systems

There are two major ideas rising in recent years for the delivery of health services, as follows:

1. The healthcare services must be structured to fulfill the needs of the entire populace and must include all types of services including preventive, curative, and rehabilitative.
2. The health service must substantially benefit the underserved rural population and urban poor to develop effective primary health care services supported by a proper recommendation system.

3.2.3 Healthcare Delivery System in India

India's healthcare system is divided into three levels: primary, secondary, and tertiary. Both governmental and commercial healthcare providers provide healthcare at these levels. However, private healthcare providers are increasingly playing a role in providing care to those who need it. "Community health centers (CHCs)", "primary health centers (PHCs)", and "sub-centers (SCs)" are all examples of primary healthcare. While sub-district hospitals are classified as secondary healthcare, district hospitals and medical colleges are classified as tertiary healthcare. The classification of the Indian healthcare system is shown in Figure 3.1; it is based on traditional health.

India is the world's second most populous country, after China, with a population of 1.21 billion people. There are eight union territories and 28 states in India. Districts and blocks are subdivided into these states and union territories. As a result, providing healthcare to such a large population has been the Indian government's greatest problem since independence. The provision of healthcare necessitates careful planning and management, as well as policies that are well-implemented and managed by government agencies in collaboration with private healthcare providers. While states are in charge of the healthcare delivery system, the center has a role to play in policymaking, planning, helping, and providing enough finances to various provincial health authorities to implement national initiatives. While the Union Ministry of "Health and Family

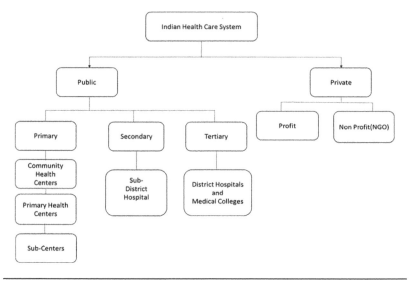

Figure 3.1   Classification of indian healthcare system.

Welfare (MOHFW)" oversees the national healthcare system, each state has its own department of Health and Family Welfare, which is led by a state minister.

The state directorate of health services devolved responsibility to each regional setup, which spans three to five districts. The middle-level health system is managed at the district level, and there is a link between the state and regional health system, also with the secondary system such as "primary health care (PHC)" and "sub-centers (SCs)".

3.2.4 Modern Healthcare Delivery System

Intelligent healthcare, fuzzy-based traffic control, smart dustbins, and automatic vehicle parking are all examples of Internet of Things (IoT) techniques. Because the patient's health is tracked via a screen, it is difficult to always evaluate the patient. As a result, sensors can be used to assess the patient's present status, such as "pulse rate", "body temperature", "body posture", "blood glucose", and "ECG". The sensors are connected to Arduino Microcontroller sensors, which collect data and send it to the server when connected to body Arduino board. The information is transferred from this website to the doctor who provides medical advice.

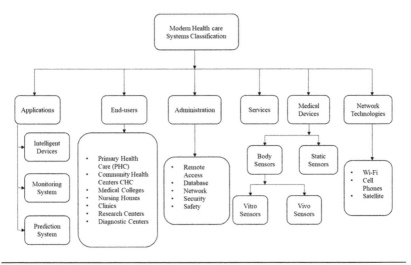

Figure 3.2   Classification of modern healthcare system.

An advanced healthcare system allows patients to be cured and improves their condition of life [7]. The e-health concept is also incorporated in the smart medical concept, which includes commands on a variety of technologies like electronic health record management, and intelligent and medically connected equipment. Sensor-based systems assist in the development of an intelligent medical system.

The classification of the modern healthcare system is shown in Figure 3.2. Artificial intelligence has been promoted in the medical sector and rapid change life. The current architecture of conventional telemedicine's science based on programming store-and-forward approach has some deficiencies:

1. A primary healthcare center with professional staff is required.
2. Medical device is necessary to compile patient data.
3. Time limit for receiving the patient data from major hospitals.
4. The expense of visiting a health center.
5. Addition of internet data usage increases.

One of the most important concerns that IoT and associated technologies must address is healthcare [14]. Collection of data via sensors and performing analysis on the collected data. There are three stages of

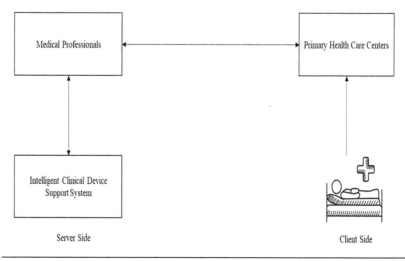

Figure 3.3   Structure of smart healthcare system.

automation based on IoT-based healthcare systems that will take decisions on health data [15]. IoT-based systems have a lot of potential for improving healthcare systems. Researchers have suggested e-health [16], community health [17], home health monitoring [18], tele-medicine [19], and digital doctor for doctors [20] as examples of healthcare applications. The major contribution of this study is the development of gadgets that aid in the monitoring, administration, and connection of many participants in the health sector.

Intelligent systems, IoT, and mobile applications are used to monitor a patient's health. Researchers can be accessed patient data at any time with the help of modern techniques. Figure 3.3 depicts the function and services of intelligent systems in the modern healthcare system. The smart healthcare system is represented as shown in Figure 3.4, Regarding ambulances with communication channels, a modern health monitoring system [21] is created and deployed. With the capabilities of low-power sensors, the Internet of Things and intelligent devices were utilized in this modern health-care system. Applications using near-field body sensor networks are thought to be a good form of communication.

A general IoT-based healthcare model is presented in this paper [22]. According to the authors, there was a one-to-one IoT-based intelligent remote patient monitoring system. It has five major sensors; three are used to monitor patient parameters such as "pulse rate", "breathing rate",

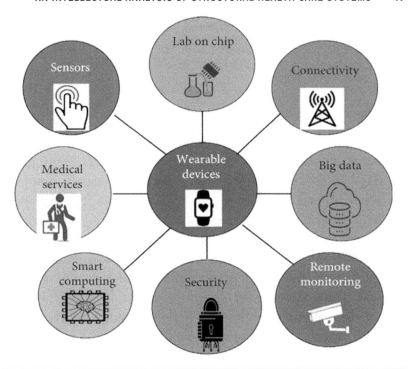

Figure 3.4 Major components of modern healthcare systems.

and "body temperature". Two sensors are utilized to keep track of "blood pressure" and "oxygen levels". In addition, the study discusses technical limitations as well as possible prospects for IoT-based remote healthcare monitoring and management systems.

The basic architecture of a sensor-based system that analyzes medical data to make fundamental decisions was put out as a viable solution. The suggested system was designed to monitor the patient's body conditions.

Designing systems for the monitoring and control of patients' health has made use of wearable body devices [23]. The study employed wearable sensors to monitor and manage patients more effectively. For this study, researchers sought out a more accurate and helpful way to collect data on patient health during surgical procedures, where human observational abilities are insufficient. There are different benefits of smaller-size equipment for patient monitoring. Fitbit health monitors, Pebble smartwatches, and Google glass are examples of the modern healthcare system. Blood pressure is an essential measurement that may be used to determine how stressed out a person's thinking is. Electronics and electrical gadgets gain an important role in human healthcare thanks to the IoT and machine learning techniques.

3.3 Structure of Intelligent Healthcare System

The recommended intelligent healthcare system makes decisions depending on the patient's circumstances. Intelligent-based technologies like IoT and artificial intelligence will manage how the sensors are utilized, as well as their cost and life span. The suggested solution tackles the issue of remote health monitoring and delivers appropriate treatment through specialists. This study describes intelligent healthcare monitoring and health control systems with integrated public and private sensors, that are supported by a single network. The recommended system is shown in Figure 3.5. In telemedicine, multiple sensors and decision support systems is an innovative approach to increase the performance of the system.

3.3.1 Data Gathering with Sensors for Intelligent Healthcare System

The proposed system would use intelligent techniques to install a gadget at a remote clinic. The gadget will communicate patients'

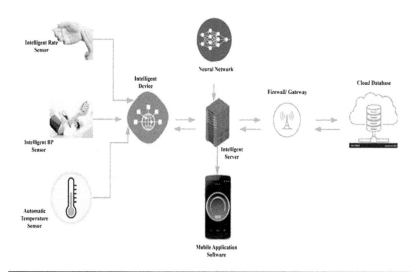

Figure 3.5   Intelligent healthcare system.

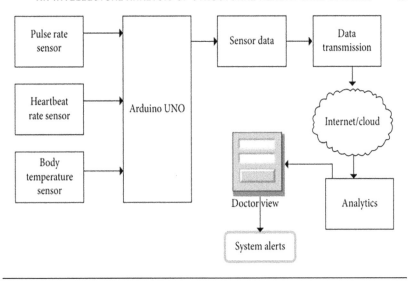

Figure 3.6   Flow of intelligent patient monitoring system.

health data to the hospital's doctor. The doctor will use the data to assess the patient's condition and advise the remote clinic personnel on the best course of action.

Figure 3.6 depicts the physical view of the components of the proposed system. The system has various sensors connected to the "Arduino Board" to gather data. Communication and networking equipment handle data transport. In this case, the intelligent system is employed to make decisions based on data analytics. The doctor's view allows hospital staff to remotely watch and engage with patients.

3.3.2 Neural Network-Based Intelligent Healthcare Monitoring and Management System

When one model is not adequate to address an issue, two or more models are integrated [24]. A hybrid system is created when several models are integrated to solve a problem. The prediction model and neural networks expressed as mixed neural networks are employed to the intelligent healthcare system.

Neural networks are designed to detect patterns, not to make decisions [25]. Probabilistic reasoning systems are effective at describing decision making, but inference rules are difficult to describe without previous information [26]. These constraints

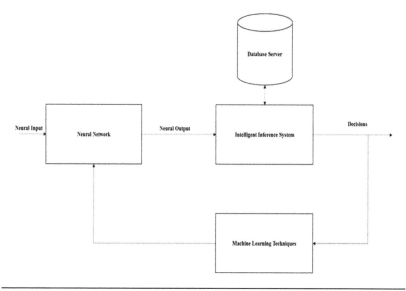

Figure 3.7   Model of neural network for the intelligent healthcare system.

gave rise to the intelligent system. Control strategies are learned from neural network patterns [27]. Figure 3.7 shows neural inputs for a neural network that produces neural outputs.

The inference rules for intelligent telemedicine:

IF ("Body Temperature == High") & ("Pulse Rate ==Low") & ("Blood Pressure == Very High")

THEN Decision =Take High Precaution

IF ("Body Temperature == High") & ("Pulse Rate == Low") & ("Blood Pressure == High")

THEN Decision = Take High Precaution

IF ("Body Temperature == Normal") & ("Pulse Rate == High") & ("Blood Pressure ==Medium")

THEN Decision = Take Normal Precautions

IF ("Body Temperature == Low") & ("Pulse Rate == High") & ("Blood Pressure ==Medium")

THEN Decision =Take Normal Precautions

IF ("Body Temperature == Normal") & ("Pulse Rate ==Normal") & ("Blood Pressure ==Low")

THEN Decision = Take High Precaution

3.3.3 Setup for Implementation

An Arduino includes four digital input/output pins. The CPU runs at 32 MHz and is powered by USB. This Arduino also has analog inputs and a reset button with an ICSP header. Arduino is an open electrical platform powered by a USB link with an output LED.

The temperature sensor detects "Heat Stroke", "Body Temperature", and "Fever". These sensors are used to measure body temperature. Inaccurate temperature sensing, "Cardiac Arrest", "Pulmonary Embolism", "Vasovagal Syncope", and "Pulse Sensor" are emergency conditions. "Pulse rate" is used to assess crucial medical and fitness problems. The "Pulse Sensor" is the most often used for patient care.

3.3.4 Experimental Results

The system is evaluated by medical professionals. The suggested gadget collects samples from several places in Lucknow. The findings are shown in the Arduino application. Table 3.1 details the areas chosen to test the suggested model. Testing will be placed in almost five places. The testing period and distance from BVH vary.

After receiving data from sensors, the electronic health record will maintain on the server. The record contains patient data, symptoms, and their procurements. The server got about 270 inquiries from specific locations. CDSS handled most of the requests. The average response time for CDSS inquiries is far faster than for physician queries.

3.3.5 Analysis of Experimental Data

The automated patient tracking system is an intelligent system that provides different facility of healthcare. The proposed system

Table 3.1 Data Collection after Experimental Setup

S. NO.	LOCATION NAME	DISTANCE FROM HOSPITALS (IN KM)	SELECTED SAMPLE	TESTING TIME
1	SGPGI	35	3	Nov 2021
2	KGMU	15	4	Dec 2021
3	ERA Medical College	20	3	Jan 2022
4	Shara Hospital	10	2	Jan 2022
5	Appolo	16	1	Feb 2022

promoted the employment of an intelligent decision-making system that is simple to use and put into action. The suggested system uses sensor data and fuzzy reasoning to make decisions. Sensor data was sent to a server through the network. In the Arduino app, we can see the results. The information that the system displays can be altered by the user. Neural networks further process the data received from the sensors and provide output.

The categories are shown in Table 3.2, there are four levels of fever (healthy, fever, high fever, and very high fever) to be classified, each corresponding to a temperature between 100°F and 105°F. As shown in Table 3.3, a typical human's pulse rate may be divided into three categories: low, normal, and high. Pulse rates lower than 64 beats per minute are referred to as low. The normal pulse rate is between 65 and 100 beats per minute. To qualify as having a high heartbeat, one must have at least 100 beats per minute.

Table 3.4 shows the different range of blood pressure. A blood pressure reading of 120/80 mm Hg is normal, 130–139/80–89 is

Table 3.2 Temperature Categories

"TEMPERATURE" (°F)	TYPE OF FEVER
"<99"	Healthy
"99–100"	Fever
"100.1–103"	High Fever
">103.1"	Very High Fever

Table 3.3 Pulse Rate Categories

"PULSE RATE" (BPM)	GROUP
">100"	High
"65–100"	Normal
"<64"	Low

Table 3.4 Blood Pressure Categories

"BLOOD PRESSURE" (HG)	GROUP
"100–110/60–70"	Low
"120/80"	Normal
"130–139/80–89"	High

Table 3.5   Data for the Examination

S. NO.	"BLOOD PRESSURE" (LOW)	"BLOOD PRESSURE" (HIGH)	"PULSE RATE" (%)	"TEMPERATURE" (°F)
1	80	120	72	99
2	94	138	70	100
3	100	180	60	101
4	88	133	107	103
5	90	136	102	105

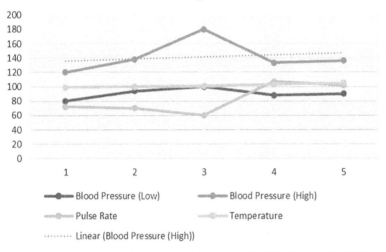

Figure 3.8   Data variations through sensors.

high and 141/91 or above is very high. Table 3.5 is use for the examination for the different parameters of health. Figure 3.8 shows the data variation through the different sensors used in experiments.

After applying the intelligent inference system, the measurement of the sensors data showed in Table 3.6. This intelligent inference system enhancing the accurateness of the proposed system. It is novel system, based on the Indian healthcare system that will revolutionarily change the medical healthcare facilities and improve the performance. Figure 3.9 and Figure 3.10 show graphical representation of the result after the analyzing the result.

Table 3.6 Measurement of Data with Intelligent Inference System

S. NO.	"TEMPERATURE"	"PULSE RATE"	"BLOOD PRESSURE"	INTELLIGENT INFERENCE SYSTEM	"ACCURACY" (%)	"ERROR" (%)
1	Low	Very High	Medium	Low	88.3	11.7
2	High	Low	Very High	High	96.9	3.1
3	Normal	Normal	Low	High	98.8	1.2
4	High	Low	Medium	Low	87.9	12.1
5	Normal	Normal	Low	High	89.1	10.9
6	Very High	Very Low	High	High	96.8	3.2
7	Low	High	High	High	96.7	3.3
8	High	Normal	Low	High	98.6	1.4
9	Low	High	Medium	Medium	92.7	7.3
10	Very High	Low	Medium	Low	86.5	13.5

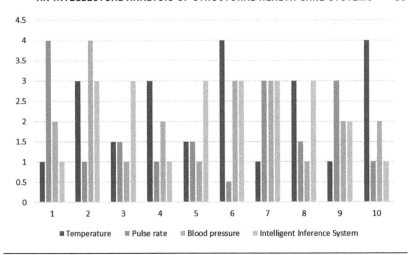

Figure 3.9   Histogram of intelligent inference system.

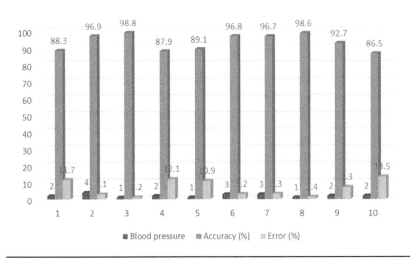

Figure 3.10   Results of accuracy based on intelligent inference system.

3.4 Conclusions and Future Work

The Indian healthcare system will change if broadly adopt the concepts of the intelligent inference system that will manage the remote location of patients and there will be different sensors are used in the whole study. Sensors for "body temperature", "blood pressure rate", and "pulse rate" are used in the proposed system to assess the state of the patients. The patient care logical learning-based system is used for automated decision-making, monitoring, and controlling to determine possible diagnoses and cures. The proposed method reduces time, cost, and labor to improve the quality of care and maintenance. In comparison to existing systems, the suggested solution handles patient intensive care with smart sensors and displays satisfactory accuracy. The study has been based on a sample group and found to be active, precise, and efficient. Therefore, the proposed technique has been broad, but it may be tailored to more urgent situations such as operating rooms, intensive care units, newborns, and more difficult patients. The result shows that the intelligent inference system will be very powerful for the medical healthcare monitoring system. In the future, we will use more sensors and fuzzy systems to diagnose the patient and get better results.

References

1. MOHFW. Annual Report 2018-2019. Available at: https://mohfw.gov.in/sites/default/files/Final%20RHS%202018-19_0.pdf (accessed on 10 January 2020).
2. How Innovations in AI, Virtual Reality are Advancing Healthcare in India to New Frontiers, J Vignes. Retrieved January 5, 2018, from http://economictimes.indiatimes.com/articleshow/59060040.cms.
3. Artificial Intelligence: Literature Review, 2017, December 16. Retrieved January 5, 2020, from https://cis-india.org/internet-governance/blog/artificial-intelligence-literature-review.
4. A. Ericson, Health AI MythBusters: Separating Fact from Fiction, 2017, October 31, Retrieved January 5, 2018, from https://www.accenture.com/us-en/blogs/blogs-health-ai-mythbusters-separating-factfiction
5. K. Safavi, The AI Will See You Now, 2016, December 15, Retrieved January 10, 2020, from https://www.accenture.com/us-en/blogs/blogs-intelligence-transform-healthcare
6. https://healthitanalytics.com/news/can-artificial-intelligence-relieve-electronic-health-recordburn
7. W. Raghupathi and V. Raghupathi, "Big data analytics in healthcare: promise and potentials," *In Health Information Science and Systems*, vol. 2, no. 1, 2014.
8. W. J. Roy and W. F. Stewart, "Prediction modelling using ehr data: challenges, strategies, and a comparison of machine learning approaches," *In Medical care*, vol. 48, no. 6, p. 106113, 2010.
9. A. Whitmore, A. Agarwal, and L. Da Xu, "+e internet of things-a survey of topics and trends," *Information Systems Frontiers*, vol. 17, no. 2, pp. 261–274, 2015.

10. P. P. Ray, "Home health hub internet of things (H3 IoT): an architectural framework for monitoring health of elderly people," in Proceedings of the 2014 International Conference on Science Engineering and Management Research (ICSEMR), pp. 1–3, Chennai, India, November 2014.

11. K. K. Goyal, A. Garg, A. Rastogi, and S. Singhal, "A literature survey on internet of things (IOT)," *International Journal of Advanced Networking and Applications*, vol. 9, no. 6, pp. 3663–3668, 2018.

12. B. K. Chae, "+e internet of things (IoT): a survey of topics and trends using twitter data and topic modelling," in Proceedings of the 22nd ITS Biennial Conference of the International Telecommunications Society (ITS): Beyond the Boundaries: Challenges for Business, Policy and Society, Seoul, South Korea, June 2018.

13. J. H. Abawajy and M. M. Hassan, "Federated internet of things and cloud computing pervasive patient health monitoring system," *IEEE Communications Magazine*, vol. 55, no. 1, pp. 48–53, 2017.

14. S. Amendola, R. Lodato, S. Manzari, C. Occhiuzzi, and G. Marrocco, "RFID technology for IoT-based personal healthcare in smart spaces," *IEEE Internet of Things Journal*, vol. 1, no. 2, pp. 144–152, 2014.

15. P. Gope and T. Hwang, "BSN-care: a secure IoT-based modern healthcare system using body sensor network," *IEEE Sensors Journal*, vol. 16, no. 5, pp. 1368–1376, 2015.

16. A.-M. Rahmani, N. K. Thanigaivelan, T. N. Gia et al., "Smart e-health gateway: bringing intelligence to Internet-of-things based ubiquitous healthcare systems," in 2015 12th Annual IEEE Consumer Communications and Networking Conference (CCNC), pp. 826–834, Las Vegas, NV, USA, 2015.

17. Y. Liu, J. Niu, L. Yang, and L. Shu, "EB Platform: An IoT-based system for NCD patients' homecare in China," in Proceedings of the 2014 IEEE Global Communications Conference, pp. 2448–2453, Austin, TX, USA, December 2014.

18. H. N. Saha, N. F. Raun, and M. Saha, "Monitoring patient's health with smart ambulance system using internet of things (IOTs)," in Proceedings of the 2017 8th Annual Industrial Automation and Electromechanical Engineering Conference (IEMECON), pp. 91–95, Bangkok, Thailand, August 2017.

19. X. M. Zhang and N. Zhang, "An open, secure and flexible platform based on internet of things and cloud computing for ambient aiding living and telemedicine," in Proceedings of the 2011 International Conference on Computer and Management (CAMAN), pp. 1–4, Wuhan, China, May 2011.

20. M. Hassanalieragh, A. Page, T. Soyata et al., "Health monitoring and management using internet-of-things (IoT) sensing with cloud-based processing: opportunities and challenges," in Proceedings of the 2015 IEEE International Conference on Services Computing, pp. 285–292, New York City, NY, USA, June 2015.

21. P. Sundaravadivel, S. P. Mohanty, E. Kougianos, V. P. Yanambaka, and H. Thapliyal, "Exploring human body communications for IoT enabled ambulatory health monitoring systems," in Proceedings of the 2016 IEEE International Symposium on Nanoelectronics and Information Systems (iNIS), pp. 17–22, Gwalior, India, December 2016.

22. S. B. Baker, W. Xiang, and I. Atkinson, "Internet of things for smart healthcare: technologies, challenges, and opportunities," *IEEE Access*, vol. 5, pp. 26521–26544, 2017.

23. D. Metcalf, S. T. J. Milliard, M. Gomez, and M. Schwartz, "Wearables and the internet of things for health: wearable, interconnected devices promise more efficient and comprehensive health care," *IEEE Pulse*, vol. 7, no. 5, pp. 35–39, 2016.

24. H. Sattar, I. S. Bajwa, and U. F. Shafi, "An intelligent air quality sensing system for open-skin wound monitoring," *Electronics*, vol. 8, no. 7, Article ID 801, 2019.

25. C.-T. Lin and C. S. G. Lee, "Neural-network-based fuzzy logic control and decision system," *IEEE Transactions on Computers*, vol. 40, no. 12, pp. 1320–1336, 1991.

26. O. Nelles, *Nonlinear System Identification: From Classical Approaches to Neural Networks and Fuzzy Models*, Springer Science & Business Media, Berlin, Germany, 2013.

27. J.-S. R. Jang, "ANFIS: adaptive-network-based fuzzy inference system," *IEEE Transactions on Systems, Man, and Cybernetics*, vol. 23, no. 3, pp. 665–685, 1993.

4

A Secure Medical-IoT Device for Assisting the Visually Impaired in External Navigation Using a Portable Braille Pad

DIVYANSH KHANDELWAL,
RISHIRAJ SINGH CHHABRA, AND
SUMIT KUMAR JINDAL

Vellore Institute of Technology,
Tamil Nadu, India

Abstract

Braille is a form of writing system that was introduced in 1824 to assist blind people to read texts and understand literature to a greater extent. Since then, innovations and advancements are being poured in to further enhance the experience of blind people and make their life better. This work presents a novel IoT-based solution that incorporates machine-to-machine communication to an electronic braille pad that a blind person can use for external navigation. The main advancement brought by this research is the fact that this device is portable and very versatile in terms of compatibility. The proposed system incorporates a mesh of radio beacons to be placed in an outdoor environment, at key and strategic positions which would publish relevant information to the braille devices when within the range. The beacon is a one-time installment that is capable of extracting data from the cloud and processing it from visually readable language to braille. This processed information is then sent across to the electronic braille pad, which acts as a client and receives the data. The data is then displayed on the braille pad with the help of micro actuators.

DOI: 10.1201/9781003269168-4

4.1 Introduction

The Internet of Things, or IoT, refers to the trillions of personal devices in the globe that are instantly connected to the net, gathering and sharing information. It refers to the connection of physical objects, such as sensors and actuators, with computers and other electronic devices over a network. The term *IoT* is used to refer both to the technology that enables these connections (e.g., sensor networks) as well as the connected things themselves (e.g., smart appliances). The most common type of IoT application in biomedical research involves connecting laboratory equipment with smartphones or tablets so that researchers can monitor data from their experiments remotely and share results with colleagues without having to visit lab sites every day.

An IoT platform allows you to connect your devices without having any knowledge about programming languages or hardware components. It provides a unified framework for developers and users alike so they can easily integrate different types of devices into their applications without worrying about how they work individually. An IoT platform also enables businesses and organizations to build intelligent solutions that leverage the power of cloud computing while reducing costs by eliminating unnecessary infrastructure requirements such as servers, routers, switches, etc … This helps companies save money on operations while increasing productivity levels by making it easier for employees at all levels within an organization to access critical data from anywhere in the world via mobile phones or tablets using simple web-based interfaces. For example, this could involve using smartphone apps like LabView Real-Time or OpenLabView Mobile to control instruments in a remote lab by sending commands via Bluetooth or Wi-Fi directly from a tablet computer running these applications, rather than having scientists manually operate controls on-site through keyboards and mouse pads while they are away from their labs. Another example would be using mobile phones equipped with sensors such as accelerometers, magnetometers, gyroscopes, or cameras that allow users to collect biological samples at home and send them back for analysis at another location—a process known as "remote sample collection"—without ever leaving home. Portable IoT devices are small, battery-powered devices that can be easily moved from place to place. They may have a built-in display or they may connect to a smartphone via Bluetooth or Wi-Fi. These devices are often used in the home, but because of their size and low power requirements, they can also be used for outdoor applications such as monitoring your garden at night using motion sensors.

The main reason why you want to use these devices is if you need an easy way to monitor something without having to install anything on your computer or phone. For example, if you want to keep track of how many people visit your house during the day when you're not there then this could be a great solution for you. If someone breaks into your house while it's dark out then this might give them away before they even get inside! Another good application is if you have pets that like going outside and don't come back in so easily after being let out by themselves (like dogs). You could set up motion sensors around the yard so that when it detects movement outside it will notify you via text message about what happened!

Thanks to low-cost processors and wireless networks, it's likely to take anything, from the tablet to the airplane, into part of the IoT. This brings the level of digital information to devices that could be otherwise slow, enabling them to interact without the person being needed, and combining the digital and physical worlds. Most of these webs were planned for client-server applications working on non-virtualized infrastructures. As most of these corporations are going towards virtualized infrastructures, including cloud, and mobility. The care business worldwide is experiencing large change. Concerns at soaring healthcare costs, effective care of chronically sick and rural patients, and the necessity for early discovery of diseases have all resulted in the noticeable change in IoT designs and their rapid acceptance over the last few years and today, these limits of conventional networking architectures are starting to grow. Although the origins of SDN date back to 1995, it wasn't until the early 21st century that SDN earned mainstream attention.

IoT has proven highly effective in its ability to churn out piles of information. Where it stands to change, and which can be the area of emphasis in 2022, is its analytical capabilities. Learning how to obtain thought from these people and zeroes as they pour in and, more importantly, do on the knowledge while it is yet applicable, can take that challenge many businesses begin to tackle in 2022.

Wearable technologies, including cell phones, are compatible with a plethora of codes like pulse monitors, cameras, and touch/pressure detectors. If gaming developers and publishers were to interact, using IoT, with these devices they'd move the new area of important information about their clients. A couple of years back, the best that the application had to give were timers. Nowadays, thanks to intelligent IoT solutions, one may get everything set up perfectly with one touch on the surface.

Industrial IoT (IIoT) is a concept that refers to the integration of sensors, actuators, and other devices into industrial systems. These systems are connected via the Internet of Things (IoT) in order to enable real-time communication and control between machines, people, and data centers. IoT is the use of connected devices to collect and exchange data, including healthcare-related information. The term *IoT* refers to a broad range of technologies that are used for collecting, processing, analyzing, and sharing data across different types of networks (both local and wide areas) to provide real-time insights into the health status or behavior of individuals or populations. The most common form of IoT in healthcare is the collection and analysis by sensors embedded within medical devices such as blood pressure monitors, glucose meters, or insulin pumps. These sensors can be programmed to send an alert when they detect abnormalities in their users' vital signs. Other forms include smartwatches with built-in fitness trackers; mobile applications that help patients manage chronic conditions; wearable devices that monitor heart rate variability; smartphone apps that allow patients to communicate with their doctors remotely via text messaging; and even "smart pillows" designed specifically for sleep monitoring. One example is a smart pillow called My Pillow that uses wireless technology to collect data about its users' sleeping habits so it can recommend better sleep positions based on how well you're sleeping at night. Another example is Smart Pillow's SleepScore app, which helps people who suffer from insomnia get better quality sleep by giving them personalized advice on how best to improve their sleep patterns through daily feedback reports sent directly from the pillow itself.

The basic idea behind IIoT is that companies can use their existing assets to improve business processes by collecting data from these assets and using this information for decision-making purposes. This means that IIoT applications can be deployed without significant changes or redesigns of current infrastructure. Instead, they rely on existing hardware like sensors or actuators as well as software solutions such as analytics platforms or cloud services. The main advantage of this approach is that it enables businesses to reduce costs while improving efficiency at the same time since only minimal investments need to be made in new equipment and software components. In addition, IIoT allows companies to make better decisions based on more accurate data since they will have access not only to historical but also real-time information about their assets. However, there are some potential issues associated with implementing IIoT solutions: security concerns related to cyber-attacks could limit how much companies can benefit from these technologies; privacy concerns regarding how personal information will be used could also affect adoption rates; finally, there might not be enough skilled personnel available who understand how these technologies work in the practice, which would limit the number of benefits gained through implementation efforts.

Cloud IoT is a new term that describes the ability to use cloud technology in order to connect, monitor, and control devices. It's not just about connecting things; it's about being able to do so from anywhere on earth. It's also about making sure that these connections are secure and reliable. The idea is that you can access all of your connected devices at any time, regardless of where you are or what device you have with you. What does this mean? Well, imagine if we could simply log into our home thermostat from wherever we were in the world at any time? Or if we could see how much power was being used by each of our appliances around the house? Or even better, if there was an alert system when something went wrong with one of those appliances (like a water heater breaking down). This type of connectivity is already happening today via smart meters and other types of sensors that can send data back to centralized data centers for analysis or manipulation. But now imagine having all this information available everywhere, anytime without needing a smartphone or computer nearby! Cloud computing is a new way of thinking about IT. It's a model that enables us to provide the software, services, and data we need when we need them—from anywhere in the world.

What does this mean? It means you can get access to your files, applications, and data from any device with an internet connection – whether it be your laptop or tablet, smartphone, or desktop computer. You don't have to worry about where you store these things because they're stored on our secure servers across multiple locations around the globe. This allows for real-time collaboration between people all over the world without having to worry about high latency issues like long-distance transmission delays or bandwidth restrictions!

Edge computing is a new approach to computing that focuses on the edge of networks. It's about using data and analytics in real-time to make better decisions, deliver more value, and improve the customer experience. The term "edge" refers to the network between your servers (the center) and end users (the edge). The idea behind edge computing is that it helps you reduce costs by offloading processing power from central locations where it's expensive to run, like data centers. This allows companies to leverage their existing infrastructure while still delivering valuable services at a lower cost. In other words, edge computing makes use of all available resources – including your own servers – so you can get more done with less money spent on hardware and software licenses.

Edge computing isn't just limited to server farms; it also applies when analyzing sensor data or IoT devices in real time for improved decision-making or predictive maintenance. For example, if you want an automated system that can detect potential problems before they happen instead of after they occur, then edge computing could be what you need!

M2M (machine-to-machine) communication is a type of machine-to-machine (M2M) communication that enables the transfer of data between two or more devices. The primary use cases for M2M include remote monitoring and control, asset tracking, vehicle tracking, and fleet management. The main benefit of using M2M technology is that it can save time by automating routine tasks such as monitoring energy consumption in buildings or vehicles. It also allows companies to monitor their assets remotely, which reduces costs associated with managing assets manually. This includes reducing labor costs and improving productivity while increasing safety measures through automatic alerts on equipment problems or maintenance needs.

MQTT is a lightweight publish/subscribe messaging protocol. It is designed to be very efficient and scalable, especially in the context of sensor networks. MQTT is an open standard that was originally developed by IBM and has been further developed by the Internet of Things (IoT) community as part of the IETF's IoT Architecture Working Group. MQTT uses TCP as its transport layer protocol which means that it provides a reliable delivery service for messages sent over IP networks such as Ethernet or Wi-Fi connections without requiring acknowledgments from the receiver before each message is delivered, unlike UDP, which does not provide this guarantee for messages sent across unreliable networks such as wireless links or cellular modems where packet loss may occur at any time because there are no acknowledgments provided by the network layer when packets are lost or corrupted during transmission.

This allows MQTT to scale to large numbers of devices with minimal overhead on both sides of a connection since all data (messages) are guaranteed to be delivered reliably even if there are many nodes connected on one network segment, whereas with UDP you would have to check every single packet individually against its destination address to determine whether or not they were received successfully before sending them out again over another link towards their final destination node(s). In addition, since MQTT uses TCP instead of UDP it provides better security features than other similar protocols due to being able to send authentication information along with each message using SSL/TLS encryption so that only authorized clients will be able to receive these messages while preventing eavesdropping attacks between unauthorized users who might try intercepting your data stream in transit without your knowledge via sniffing packets between your device and its server(s).

4.2 Overview of the Problem

4.2.1 Theory

Communication is the key to societal development and plays a major role in the growth of any community or civilization. Since the tech revolution, our ways of communication have exponentially improved: from diode valves to billions of transistors in a square inch of space.

These innovations affected the masses and built a great economy of countries but what they did not achieve was a comprehensive binding of communities [1]. Communication for the blind is a system of communication that allows people who are visually impaired to communicate with others. It can be used in many different ways: written, spoken, or sign language. Communication for the blind can also help individuals learn how to read and write braille. People with disabilities are found to be the worst sufferers when it comes to technological advancements that assist them in day-to-day life. It is necessary to provide them with information and make our communities as inclusive as we can so that we do not leave out slim margins of society. Braille is a necessary tool for all visually impaired people as braille serves as the only medium for them to read and write.

Yet there is an alarming illiteracy among visually impaired individuals. Statistics point towards a less than 10% literacy rate among children who are visually impaired [2]. Therefore, if one works towards increasing the chances of these children and makes amendments to bring more acceptance in society for visually impaired individuals, we need to bring about a change. There has been near no aid for a blind person if he/she decides to get groceries from the market. Therefore, this proposition would bring revolutionary changes in their day-to-day life.

Commercially available braille pads are too bulky and not portable at all. These devices were meant to be used in educational institutes for the visually impaired and are only devised to be present in the room itself. The cost of these devices is also skyrocketing. A standard braille machine costs about $3000 to $5000, which becomes a huge challenge when it comes to accessibility. All these factors are hence taken into consideration and are worked upon in this research. The proposed work is developing a portable handheld refreshable braille pad that will primarily be used for indoor navigation assistance for people with disabilities. The focus of the work is to assist deaf and blind people to find key locations in a campus or indoor facility with the help of a lightweight and portable braille pad, based on the principles of magnetic solenoid actuators, hypertext transfer protocol (HTTPS) and message queuing and telemetry transport (MQTT). The work employs the use of cloud databases and Node MCU as beacons and main processors of the braille pad. The database will be deployed on the cloud and the WiFi beacons will be in sync with the database for real-time over-air (OTA) updates. Thus, this system ensures a secure way of communication between multiple devices and safe transfer of messages.

4.2.2 Braille Language

Braille was developed by a French educator named Louis Braille. Braille is a tactile writing system that is read by touch. It was developed in France in the early 1800s and has been adapted to be used on computers, cell phones, and other devices. Braille uses six raised dots to represent letters of the alphabet. The dots are arranged in two parallel rows of three dots each. Each letter or number has its unique pattern of dots so that it can be identified easily when reading text with braille embossers or computer software such as screen readers for people who are blind or visually impaired. Louis Braille invented a method of writing and reading that can be interpreted by visually impaired individuals and this language was named after him, called braille.

Braille can be easily understood by breaking it down into its building blocks. Each braille character is represented by a braille cell. A braille cell is shown in Figure 4.1, and can be considered the building block of the braille system. There is then a mapping of common languages to braille language wherein each alphabet the character of that language is uniquely represented by the combinations of braille dots in which raised dots represent the letters of the alphabet. The important thing to understand is that braille is not a language, it is a translation/representation of other languages encoded in these braille cells and dots which allow visually impaired individuals the ability to read. Braille is written from left to right, top to bottom, just like it's read. To write braille, you need special

Figure 4.1 Braille cell.

Table 4.1   Braille Parameters [4]

BRAILLE PARAMETERS	ACCEPTABLE LENGTH IN INCHES
Dot Base Diameter	0.059 to 0.063
Distance between two dots in the same cell	0.090 to 0.100
Distance between corresponding dots in adjacent cells	0.241 to 0.300
Dot height	0.025 to 0.037
Distance between corresponding dots from one cell directly below	0.395 to 0.400

equipment that includes a stylus (a small stick with an ink tip) and paper with raised dots on it. You can also use your fingers if you're writing by hand instead of using the stylus. There are two main ways to write braille: print braille and computer braille, both of which have different symbols for letters and numbers. Print braille uses the same symbols as English braille but without any punctuation marks or spaces between words; computer braille also has these extra characters but they don't appear in print, so they're not needed when reading text on computers or mobile devices such as smartphones and tablets.

4.2.3 Braille Cell

A braille cell consists of six individually addressable dots that give a total of 64 permutations. These dots are arranged in a 2 × 3 matrix and any of the dots can be raised. Table 4.1 describes the set guidelines by the Braille Authority [3] that need to be followed.

4.3 Literature Survey

Braille is a communication method for people with visual impedances who use it to communicate. The main focus is on a novel plan of an easy, low-force, convenient, and easy-to-understand braille framework. This technology can be used to read, write, and communicate. The work done employs the use of optical character recognition (OCR) in Python to detect the text written in a PDF and then display it on an LCD screen and a braille box [5].

Optical character recognition, or OCR, is a technology for recognizing characters from a digital image using computer vision.

OCR works by analyzing the light and dark patterns in the image that form letters and numbers to convert the image into text. OCR can recognize letters and numbers in different fonts, so rules are used to help the system align what they see in an image with the correct letters or numbers. Optical character recognition has existed in the technological world for decades now but has recently started to use in a variety of applications. One such application is to convert text to braille using an image-capturing device like a camera, scanner, etc. The recognized characters are then mapped to a database of predefined key-value pairs and converted into braille. Solenoids are used to actuate or replicate braille patterns physically [6].

The drawback of this system is that it's not portable and the LCD of braille characters is of no use to the visually impaired person that is using this system. The result of this system is that it is not portable and the LCD for braille characters is of no use to the blind person who is using this system.

Since communication is the most important aspect of human existence, it gets really difficult for people with audio and visual disabilities when it comes to communication. The traditional ways of communication include sign language and braille but they come with their own set of constraints e.g., being in the line of sight for the sign language and having a permanent physical object to communicate via braille. A possible solution to this problem is to have a refreshable braille screen that transforms text information from a computer to the corresponding braille representation for visually impaired individuals [7]. This technology uses micro-vibration motors that are secured on the person's body the act as braille actuators. Experimental results show that while testing this system on PWD, it took 0.5–1.4 seconds for the braille pad to refresh and convert the transmitted signals from SMS to motor signals. This latency in the system is too much for a PWD to maintain the flow of communication.

A communication system was published in 2013 where the research was based on communication between blind or deaf people with the help of the SMS subsystem [8]. People with visual impairments tend to face a lot of hardships relating to easy access to information. The current braille displays in the market have something between 8 and 80 cells and are increasing.

A major factor for concern is the non-availability of specific software which can be adapted to users' needs. A possible solution is to develop a single braille unit since braille is read character by character. The solution would also consist of software that is integrated with the hardware solution. This software would use the accessibility standards laid down by the U.S. Consortium for people with visual impairments [9].

Touch is a really important way of communication for people with visual impairments. One of the ways this mode of communication can be used to make it easier for them to converse is to have a glove with actuators placed on the fingertips of the middle finger, index finger, and ring finger which represents the six dots in braille. The solution could also convert all Bengali characters efficiently [10].

Self-learning is probably the best way to learn anything and that ignites the idea of developing a self-learning braille kit. The device is proposed to have two modes of operation. The first mode is modulated as a learning mode, consisting of six solenoid actuators. The second mode is devised as a practice mode. This mode allows the user to practice the accuracy of the braille characters with some exercises [11].

Since the braille dots are really small in size and to replicate the braille design, motors, and other electronic components would have to be in micro-scale, it would be important for MEMS-based braille systems to come into existence. Being on a micro-scale would also result in reduced voltage requirements, which would be beneficial for the battery life of the hardware. The solution will be able to convert digital text files into tactile signals using a USB port [12].

To develop a tactile wearable system, vibrotactile assistance is used for communication based on braille using fingers which is a method used by people with disabilities. It is made using flexible piezo-resistive material whereas the actuator works on the electromagnetic principle and NdFeB permanent magnet [13]. Shape memory is one of the ways for information to be conveyed to people with visual impairments. One such material is shape memory alloy (SMA) wire. The feature that allows the transition from the martensite phase to the austenite phase, is the temperature can change the dimensions of the alloy. The braille characters can be replicated by these SMA by varying the temperature in a very calculated way. Depending on the optimal displacement, these actuators can be used to vibrate to stimulate human tactile sensation [14].

Another solution for assisting PWD is by using touch screens. Using touch screens becomes difficult for people with visual impairments because the whole touch screen surface is even and there is no way to notify the user where exactly to make contact with the screen. The screen and the system are also not portable, thus making it not suitable for navigation purposes. This problem can be tackled using deep learning algorithms that are much more efficient in front of the machine learning algorithms such as support vector machine (SVM) or K-nearest neighbor (KNN) as mentioned in this research [15].

4.4 System Model

Figure 4.2 explains the system architecture of the electronic braille pad model. There are three major layers in the architecture diagram

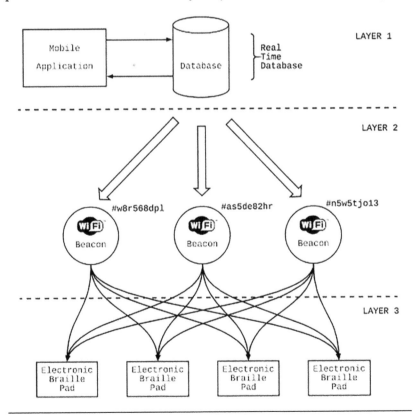

Figure 4.2   The system architecture of IoT braille pad.

which constitute both hardware and software layers of the model. The top layer is the cloud layer and the application layer. In this layer sits the database and the mobile application that is meant for the system admin to use. For every outdoor building, there will be a network of strategic places, for instance, take an example of a university. In a university, there are many buildings, and different routes leading to different buildings, blocks, hostels, etc. Inside the academic building, there will be even more strategic locations like the canteen, washroom, classrooms, lifts, stairs, water cooler, etc. All these key locations will be mapped and marked by the admin. These strategic locations are places where a person would want to go and where a person with visual impairment would want to be directed. The mesh of these locations will be equipped with Wi-Fi beacons that will be placed and secured there. The role of these beacons is to broadcast a public message to all the nearby subscribers.

Since the braille pad model is portable, it becomes extremely easy to scale it from indoor navigation to outdoor navigation. The unique feature of this system is that it is widely scalable because these key locations can be mapped easily by the admin. The admin then uses the key locations which they selected and enters a particular message for each of these key locations. This can be understood by an example, a message of "Stairs to the 6th floor in 10 meters towards the right" can be linked to a position where there is a flight of stairs leading from the 5th floor to the 6th floor. Similarly, with a message like "Road crossing approaching 20 meters, take right for the metro station". Now the great feature of the proposed system is that all these messages are customizable by the admins or the system in charge. That implies the admin who is installing the system in their premises has total control over the system, the mesh of locations, the message to be broadcasted, etc.

The second layer in the architecture is the Wi-Fi beacon layer. In this layer, all the beacons will be configured which will hold a unique identification code attached to them. This unique ID will be used to map the message entered by the admin to the beacon that is placed corresponding to the location it will be installed. These beacons will be equipped with a Wi-Fi gateway which allows them to get real-time updates from the cloud. These beacons act as an access point to other braille pads in the vicinity. All nearby braille pads in a radius of 10 meters from the beacon can subscribe to it and receive the message.

The communication protocols which have been used in the model are hypertext transfer protocol (HTTP) and message queuing telemetry transport (MQTT). As evident from the architecture diagram, the middle layer needs to be connected to both the first layer and the second layer. For safe communication between the database and the Wi-Fi beacons, we have used the HTTPS protocol. Since HTTP protocol is a reliable way of communication and comes out of the box with a Wi-Fi-enabled microcontroller, hence it is best suited for this application. For the communication between the second layer and the third layer, that is between the beacon and the electronic braille pad, the system uses MQTT protocol for the transfer of braille data. As shown in Figure 4.2, communication requires many to many protocols. The architectural requirements were of a publisher-subscriber-based model where the publisher can publish the message to the braille device and the braille pad can then display that message. Thus, for the same reason, MQTT was best suited for this application when it was required to communicate between the beacon and the braille pad. In this model, each of the numerous beacons placed will act as a publisher node which will have a message assigned to it and will then communicate it to the braille pad.

4.5 Architecture Specification and Implementation

4.5.1 Software Stack

4.5.1.1 Database For databases, the model uses firebase real-time database or RTDB. In RTDB, the data is stored in a JavaScript object notation (JSON) format, as shown in Figure 4.3. A real-time database like RTDB is a database framework that utilizes real-time preparation to deal with outstanding burdens whose state is continually changing. This varies from conventional databases containing relentless information, generally unaffected by time. For instance, the financial exchange changes quickly and is dynamic. The diagrams of the various business sectors seem, by all accounts, to be truly insecure but then a database needs to monitor current qualities for the entirety of the business sectors of the New York Stock Exchange.

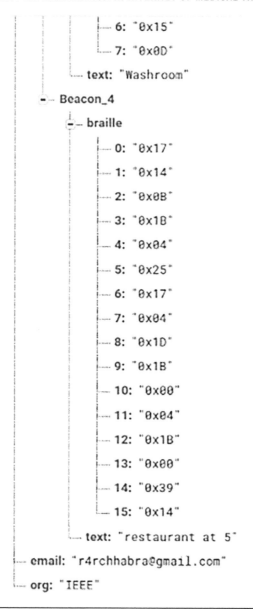

Figure 4.3 JSON data in firebase Real-Time Database (RTDB).

The real-time database works in JavaScript object notation format. It is a popular and industry-accepted way of representing data and is widely used to transfer data. It is a lightweight model for formatting, storing, and transporting data over the web and is widely used when any data packet is communicated between a server and a client. The database structure used for braille pads is as shown in Figure 4.3.

In the JSON object, there is a unique user ID (UUID) for every beacon, and corresponding to it is the necessary information regarding the beacon. The message is stored in two formats, one format in English, which is stored by the admin while inserting the message via app and in the second format the message is stored in an array of strings that contains the hexadecimal value. This hexadecimal value is a mapping generated by a serverless cloud function that runs on firebase and converts the English test message to a machine-equivalent hex value. These hexadecimal values are then read by the beacon and are used to actuate the array on single-addressable braille cells present in the braille pad. The outermost collection consists of three fields:

1. Counter
2. Devices
3. Users

The "counter" is an integer value that indicates the number of devices in the organization. The "devices" consist of beacon data. The beacon data consists of four fields:

1. Message data
2. orgName – Organization Name
3. Braille data
4. userName

4.5.1.2 Mobile Application   The mobile application is made using Flutter. Flutter is Google's UI toolkit for building beautiful, natively compiled applications for mobile, web, and desktop from a single codebase.

The app, as seen in Figure 4.4, is broadly divided into two categories:

1. UI Component: The UI components include everything that the user can see. For e.g., the List View of cards in the active devices section and the Add a device button. The app consists of three pages, 1) Login Page, 2) Onboarding Organization page, and 3) Dashboard.

Figure 4.4   HERE mobile application screen.

The login page consists of a Sign in with Google button. When this button is pressed the app makes HTTP calls to the Google OAuth2 REST APIs and authenticates the user. Upon successful authentication, Google returns the user data such as username, user email etc.

2. CRUD Operation: CRUD or Create Read Update and Delete operation is done concerning a database when a value is stored, read, updated, or deleted in front of the database.

After the user has been authenticated, the app does a Create operation by making a new user field in the real-time database consisting of userName, user email, and organization name. When the user is redirected to the dashboard, the app performs a Read operation to get all the existing beacons and their data from the RTDB.

4.5.1.3 User Experience
1. Register into the app using Google Account.

2. Enter the organization name during onboarding for the first time.
3. The user will be able to see all the active beacons with their messages.
4. They can edit the message and delete the beacon from the same screen.
5. The admin can add a new beacon by pressing the "Add a device" button.
6. The next screen will ask for the Beacon name and the message to be attached to the particular beacon.
7. On pressing add, the flutter app will convert each character of the message in English to a Hexadecimal Code.
8. This list of Hex codes along with the actual message in English will be stored in the database along with the beacon name and the organization name.

4.5.2 Hardware Stack

For hardware implementation, the model uses an ESP8266 microcontroller as the brains of both the beacon and the braille pad. Specifications of esp8266 are mentioned in Table 4.2.

For the braille pad actuators, the microcontroller is connected to a series of micro linear actuators. These actuators are based on the principle of electromagnetic induction. Each of the actuators is a small solenoid that acts as an inductor and induces a magnetic field in the iron core. This induced magnetic field thus has a magnetic polarity and creates a temporary magnet inside the core. Above the solenoid, a magnet is placed that is aligned in the same polarity as the solenoid. When the microcontroller sends the HIGH value to the solenoid, 5 V DC voltage is applied across, which flows sufficient

Table 4.2   Specifications of Node MCU

DEVICE FEATURE	SPECIFICATION
CPU	80 MHz 32-bit
Dynamic RAM	128 KB
Flash Memory	4 MB
WiFi	2.4 GHz 802.11 b/g/n
Serial I/O	Micro USB

current to generate a magnetic field capable of repelling the permanent magnet by a distance of 0.5 mm. This is how linear actuation is achieved in the braille pad. One other issue that was faced during the development of the braille pad was to find a method to actuate about 300 microactuators with the least amount of possible pins. If the braille pad needs to display five lines of braille characters and each line contains 10 braille characters, then this amounts to 300 actuators in total, which is not possible if every actuator was connected to a separate pin on the microcontroller. Thus, to solve this issue, the model uses serial in parallel out shift registers, which can be connected in progression and parallelly actuate eight actuators at a time. 74HC595 Shift Register is an 8-bit serial-in parallel-out (SIPO) register that takes in serial data bytes and outputs these bytes parallelly to 8 pins on the IC. The Q0-Q7 pins are the parallel output pins that are connected to linear actuators. DS is the data pin that inputs serial data to the shift register from the microcontroller.

4.5.3 Hardware Implementation

The beacon uses the "firebaseesp8266" client library provided by firebase to integrate with the firebase API to perform CRUD operations on the real-time database. In the configuration of the beacon, primarily the beacon initiates the local wi-fi connection. On initiating the Wi-Fi connection, the firebase client-side SDK is configured and initiated, which allows reading the braille data in form of the JSON object.

The data is coded in a way that represents the pins in each braille cell. The pins of the braille cells are marked from 0 to 5 in a clockwise direction starting from the top left. After this, the pin that needs to be high is marked one and the rest are marked low. This results in a sequence of ones and zeros. This sequence is then placed in a data frame of a byte such that the 0th bit corresponds to the 0th pin of a braille cell and so on. The 6th and the 7th pin is left blank, which is used to map the braille cells internally in the microprocessor.

Therefore with this method, a braille cell can be represented by a byte and thus an array of bytes can store a particular message. Figure 4.5 shows the response of the HTTP call made by the beacon

```
"devices": {
    "Beacon_3": {
        "braille": [
            "0x3A",
            "0x04",
            "0x0B",
            "0x16",
            "0x17",
            "0x15",
            "0x15",
            "0x0D"
        ],
        "text": "Washroom"
    },
    "Beacon_4": {
        "braille": [
            "0x17",
            "0x14",
            "0x0B",
            "0x1B",
            "0x04",
            "0x25",
            "0x17",
            "0x04",
            "0x1D",
            "0x1B",
            "0x00",
            "0x04",
            "0x1B",
            "0x00",
            "0x39",
            "0x14"
        ],
        "text": "restaurant at 5"
    }
},
"email": "r4rchhabra@gmail.com",
"org": "IEEE"
```

Figure 4.5 HTTP response from the database.

to the database. This array of a byte is then transmitted to the braille pads which are in the vicinity by the MQTT transfer protocol.

Implementation of a single braille cell is demonstrated in Figure 4.6. The shift register 74hc595 is configured in the microcontroller and shown in Figure 4.6. to simulate the actuation in the software, simple 5 V LEDs are used in place of microactuators as this model is just a proof-of-concept model. Q2 to Q7 outputs are used to actuate a braille cell. The first two bits from the shift register are not used as the values are used up internally in the microcontroller for internal mapping.

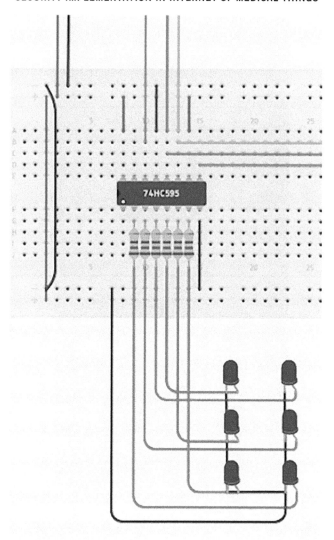

Figure 4.6   Implementation of a braille cell.

A braille row is configured in Figure 4.7. Here, multiple 74hc595 shift registers are connected in series and thus data is allowed to transmit across the chain on the shift registers. 74hc595 allows chaining multiple SIPO registers also known as daisy-chaining. The mechanism of daisy chaining is as follows: the clock pin, which is STcp, and latches pin that is SHcp are shared between all the daisy-chain 74hc595 chips while every Q7' PIN of the previous 74hc595 in the chain is used as serial

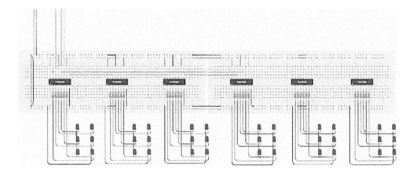

Figure 4.7   Implementation of a braille row.

input for the next chip in the chain. This method of daisy-chaining allows connecting multiple numbers of 74HC595 IC and ensures a serial transfer of data among the individual braille cells.

4.6 Results and Discussion

The system has been designed with the help of solenoids, Node MCU, and a database. Since the application of the proposed solution is an implementation in the field of effective communication, the delay needs to be close to none. The users will be able to log into the app using their Google accounts, which then will fetch their email IDs and name from the Google account.

Figure 4.8 shows the first screen that the user is going to witness. This screen allows the user to enter the Organization Name where all

Figure 4.8   Initialize organization.

the beacons are installed. The application will then group, the user, organization, and beacons together. The data is then sent to the firebase real-time database, making representational state transfer (REST) application programming interface (API) calls to the end-points provided by the Firebase Services. Upon a successful response from the server and registration of the user and the organization, the user is redirected to the dashboard.

The dashboard shown in Figure 4.9 contains:

a. Name of the user
b. The number of active beacons
c. A list of all the beacons along with their messages

The user can then click on any beacon in the list and can make changes to existing messages. The user can also delete the beacon and reset the device by performing a "long-press" gesture on the beacon name and then selecting the "Reset" option. The same beacon can be reinitialized by using the "Add a device" button at the bottom of the screen.

Figure 4.9   Dashboard of application.

Figure 4.10   Add new device.

On clicking the button, the app will respond by showing a pop-up dialog box for the user to fill in the details mentioned in Figure 4.10. The user can then confirm the details by pressing "Add". This would send a request to the REST APIs of Firebase RTDB and will perform the create read update delete (CRUD) operation by adding a new set of data in the database. The screen will then show a green tick mark confirming that the device has been successfully added to the organization group. The beacons will now be able to communicate with the braille pad to convey the new message to the user.

4.7 Conclusion

The proposed model for IoT-enabled braille pad was able to formulate a solution to the existing problems that include effective methods of communication, better cost-to-worth ratio, and portability. The braille pad can be used by anyone with little or no practice. The proposed solution uses solenoids as microactuators for the actuation of the braille pins, mimicking the letters of the braille in a braille cell. This makes the device highly portable, accurate, and user-friendly for people with visual impairment disabilities. The proposed solution is also highly cost-effective, being about five times cheaper than the existing solutions in the market. This enables the device to be used by a larger audience.

References

[1] Shokat, S., Riaz, R., Rizvi, S. S. et al., "Deep learning scheme for character prediction with position-free touch screen-based Braille input method," *Hum. Cent. Comput. Inf. Sci.*, vol. 10, 2020, p. 41. 10.1186/s13673-020-00246-6

[2] https://brailleworks.com/braille-literacy-statistics/

[3] http://www.brailleauthority.org/sizespacingofbraille/sizespacingof braille.pdf

[4] National Library Service for the Blind and Physically Handicapped, Library of Congress.Specification 800: Braille Books and Pamphlets. loc.gov/nls/specs/800_march5_2008.pdf

[5] S. Sultana, A. Rahman, F. H. Chowdhury, and H. U. Zaman, "A novel Braille pad with dual text-to-Braille and Braille-to-text capabilities with an integrated LCD," 2017 International Conference on Intelligent Computing, Instrumentation and Control Technologies (ICICICT), Kannur, 2017, pp. 195–200, doi: 10.1109/ICICICT1. 2017.8342559.

[6] R. Sarkar, S. Das, and D. Rudrapal, "A low-cost microelectromechanical Braille for blind people to communicate with blind or deaf-blind people through SMS subsystem," 2013 3rd IEEE International Advance Computing Conference (IACC), Ghaziabad, 2013, pp. 1529–1532, doi: 10.1109/IAdCC.2013.6514454.

[7] R. Sarkar, S. Das, and D. Rudrapal, "A low-cost microelectromechanical Braille for blind people to communicate with blind or deaf-blind people through SMS subsystem," 2013 3rd IEEE International Advance Computing Conference (IACC), Ghaziabad, 2013, pp. 1529–1532, doi: 10.1109/IAdCC.2013.6514454.

[8] M. Bernard Schmidt, L. Gustavo, and A. R. G. Ramírez, "Single Braille cell," 5th ISSNIP-IEEE Biosignals and Biorobotics Conference (2014): Biosignals and Robotics for Better and Safer Living (BRC), Salvador, 2014, pp. 1–5, doi: 10.1109/BRC.2014.6880990.

[9] A. Hazra and M. M. Hoque, "Braille Gloves: An Intelligent Hand-Glove to Generate Bengali Braille Characters for Visually Impaired People," 2019 IEEE Region 10 Symposium (TENSYMP), Kolkata, India, 2019, pp. 523–528, doi: 10.1109/TENSYMP46218.2019.8971041.

[10] M. Abdul Kader, R. Ahmed, M. I. Rahman Noman, A. Billah, and M. Uddin Apple, "Developing A Self-Learning Braille Kit For Visually

Impaired People," 2018 International Conference on Innovations in Science, Engineering, and Technology (ICISET), Chittagong, Bangladesh, 2018, pp. 47–51, doi: 10.1109/ICISET.2018.8745595.

[11] M. Abdul Kader, R. Ahmed, M. I. Rahman Noman, A. Billah, and M. Uddin Apple, "Developing A Self-Learning Braille Kit For Visually Impaired People," 2018 International Conference on Innovations in Science, Engineering, and Technology (ICISET), Chittagong, Bangladesh, 2018, pp. 47–51, doi: 10.1109/ICISET.2018.8745595.

[12] H. Arshad, U. S. Khan, and U. Izhar, "MEMS based Braille system," 2015 IEEE 15th International Conference on Nanotechnology (IEEE-NANO), Rome, 2015, pp. 1103–1106, doi: 10.1109/NANO.2015.7388815.

[13] O. Ozioko, P. Karipoth, M. Hersh, and R. Dahiya, "Wearable Assistive Tactile Communication Interface Based on Integrated Touch Sensors and Actuators," in *IEEE Transactions on Neural Systems and Rehabilitation Engineering*, vol. 28, no. 6, June 2020, pp. 1344–1352, doi: 10.1109/TNSRE.2020.2986222.

[14] C. Jiang, F. Zhao, K. Uchida, and H. Sawada, "Research and development on portable Braille display using shape memory alloy wires," 2011 4th International Conference on Human System Interactions, HSI 2011, Yokohama, 2011, pp. 318–323, doi: 10.1109/HSI.2011.5937385.

[15] H. R. Choi, S. W. Lee, and K. M. Jung, "Tactile Display As A Braille Display For The Visually Disabled," *Intelligent Robots And Systems, Proceedings*, vol. 2, 2004, pp. 1985–1990.

5

CYBERSECURITY IN MEDICAL INTERNET OF THINGS

Issues, Challenges, and Future Directions

RACHANA Y. PATIL[1], YOGESH H. PATIL[2], AND APARNA BANNORE[3]

[1]*PimpriChinchwad College of Engineering, Pune, Maharashtra, India*
[2]*Dr. D. Y. Patil Institute of Technology, Pune, Maharashtra, India*
[3]*SIES Graduate School of Technology, Nerul, Navi Mumbai, India*

Abstract

The integration of the Internet and communication technologies has improved our lives in numerous ways. To date, the Internet of Things has evolved the healthcare industry from Healthcare 1.0 to 4.0 which is known as the Medical Internet of Things (MIoT). In Healthcare 4.0, data is shared among multiple stakeholders through the use of cloud computing, fog computing, and telehealth. MIoT devices and technology's interconnected, heterogeneous nature raises new concerns about access to patients' personal data, which is frequently done without patients' or medical practitioners' knowledge. This is because security and privacy concerns for MIoT instruments and technology are frequently ignored or harmed by the actions of relevant stakeholders. Medical IoT security and privacy are becoming increasingly important as a result of the increasing number of security breaches targeting the MIoT in healthcare. Many security experts and researchers have expressed concern about the MIoT's security and privacy in light of its rapid growth in recent years. With these facts as a springboard, we've conducted a comprehensive study to find the security and privacy issues, challenges, the susceptible devices in MIoT, and the future directions to keep healthcare data safe and private in the age of Industry 4.0 are all discussed.

5.1 Introduction

Technological evolvement and its integration is becoming essential part of our daily lives. The Internet of Things (IoT) plays an important role in providing smooth and seamless ubiquitous services for everyone, reducing the need for human labor, and assisting in all over the place linking everyone.

In general, smart physical objects those are interconnected along with sensors, the required software, and network connectivity, all together becomes part of the Internet of Things (IoT) [1]. Every worldwide company and consumer domain has been transformed by the Internet of Things (IoT), which is currently altering and transforming both the corporate and consumer world.

Along with healthcare and smart cities, it's also being used in agriculture and the armed forces [2–5]. As a result, the Internet of Things (IoT) has the potential to transform how individuals engage with the world. In 2020, the IoT market share was estimated around USD$761.4 billion and by 2026 it is expected to achieve USD $1386.06 billion; this indicates its global relevance as leading technology concept for increasing the welfare of millions of people [6–9].

IoT in healthcare, or Medical IoT (MIoT), describes a broad variety of IoT devices that have a primary objective to serve and support in basic patient care system [10]. It is estimated that globally the IoT in the healthcare industry would rise to USD$446.52 billion in 2028, from USD$71.84 billion in 2020.

Patients' critical body parameters and pathological data can be monitored by wearable or implantable medical sensors [11–13]. Currently, healthcare industries are opting for more modern MIoT-based products and services for treating patients, diagnosing, and managing disease with better patient care at minimum cost. A real time patient monitoring is possible from a distance using MIoT devices, and the data collected can be analyzed and sent to the cloud or medical record centers for further handling and storage prior it is made available to respective participants, like doctors, paramedical staff, and health insurance service providers [14].

A wide range of MIoT applications may be found in the field of healthcare monitoring and management. These include solutions for remote monitoring of health for geriatric patients, clinical investigation and support systems (CISS), medical prescription system, and so on. While this may be true, it's also clear that the Internet of Things (IoT) has transformed healthcare companies, allowing for the provision of services to patients at home where doctors can keep tabs on their health status while they go about their regular routines. Multiple subsystems can be created within a typical MIoT system. Figure 5.1 depicts a typical MIoT structure in healthcare as a starting point for understanding.

Medical IoT devices with a variety of smart sensors are typically found in MIoT healthcare applications. Smart gadgets are also integrated into global information networks system for easy and immediate access. Physical objects in the MIoT system can be integrated and connected to the Internet, allowing for remote access to equipment that checks, analyses, forecast, and store crucial medical information. On the other side, due to the fast-developing IoT threat

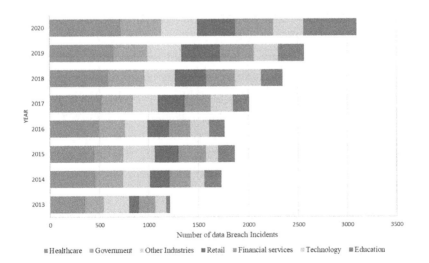

Figure 5.1   Data breach statistics according to type of industry.

environment, the interloper can exploit and way into the MIoT network for excess abuse of the overall medical system and setup.

This eventually progresses to scenarios in which the security and confidentiality of the medical devices and patient's data are in danger. If MIoT devices keep increasing in volume, they will ultimately lead to the wider disclosure of personal medical data, and it requires an added investigation [15,16]. A key issue still necessary to be addressed in healthcare is the security and privacy of data collected by MIoT devices, where business and academia aren't paying enough attention. Further, data breaching in the healthcare industry is at large as the latest statistics revels and presented in Figure 5.1.

The rapid development of IoT-based MIoT systems causes exposing the patient's personal information which is confidential and is accessible to unauthorized parties. It is possible for invaders to access the implanted or any life-supporting medical device remotely to change the critical body parameters, which is life-threatening to patients.

Furthermore, it's at high risk for patients if passive network operators could misuse patient's personal information from network traffic for marketing purposes. The lack of sufficient acquaintance regarding the security of MIoT devices and networks among end users and related stakeholders like patients and medical experts leads to intensify vulnerabilities and in many cases, attackers can take the advantage of such situations pushing patients' lives at risk [17].

It's not limited to this, but in the event of cyber-attacks, the major concerns for the healthcare industry would be data theft and loss of critical information, ultimately resulting in compromising patients' data [18]. The recent statistics of cyber-attacks in the healthcare industry shows the volume of damage, as shown in Figure 5.2. The continuous expansion of IoT-based healthcare market expects a total business turnover of USD$100 billion by 2025, this study also confirms our attempts to verify the present scenario of safety and security of MIoT.

Surprisingly, the whole world experienced a shock in November 2019 by the outbreak of a lethal virus called COVID-19 that spread very quickly to nations all over the world. It is estimated that the global population is reduced by around 4 million due to COVID-19 casualties to date and yet it's not clear about the outbreak of the next

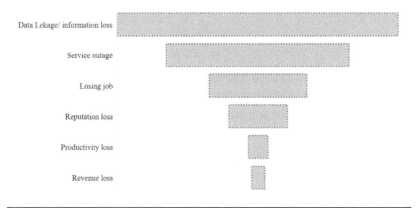

Figure 5.2 Volume of damage due to cyber-attacks in the healthcare industry.

variants of COVID-19 viruses and their severity, diagnosis, and management. Possible measures like imposing complete or partial lockdown, night curfews, and restrictions on public gatherings; social functions are implemented to control the spread of this fatal disease. MIoT played a crucial role during this COVID pandemic while working with government agencies, various NGOs, and healthcare institutes for monitoring the disease. With the COVID virus being contagious, the life of the treating medical team is at risk, and remote patient tracking, monitoring, and management is essential and becomes possible due to MIoT technology. There is a huge surge in demand for MIoT-based applications and devices during the COVID pandemic period and ultimately the incidences of cyber threats increased as per the literature [19,20], which encourages the study in this domain.

5.2 Motivation

MIoT assures the excellence in the healthcare management system, and this leads to the well-being of society as a whole and hence it's the indirect way of contributing for nation-building. If counter-measures are not initiated at the right time, the MIoT system will suffer from a lot of malfunctioning, and patient data and lives will be at risk.

At the same time, with the tremendous expansion of MIoT-based healthcare applications and services in recent years, it is essential to address security and privacy issues. As time advances, lots of researchers and suppliers are working presently towards the consolidation of security and privacy features of MIoT system, making it faithful and robust [21,22]. However, with MIoT being the novel technology, current research assignments are in their initial phase as a concern to data security and privacy. As a result, this inspires us to write this chapter is an effort for better understanding along with compiling the existing state of facts about security and privacy of MIoT and to open up new avenues for researcher scholars, academia, and interested suppliers in these topics to do additional research.

5.3 MIoT Architecture

The primary purpose of this chapter is to review and identify the current status of data privacy and its security related to MIoT. Initially it is necessary to understand the basic functioning of devices used and its fundamental architecture that is applied to develop the framework for the detail understanding of different privacy and security issues and their severity. Thus, in this section, our main focus is to discuss the framework of MIoT and devices used in individual layers of the framework. Figure 5.3 shows the basic structure of MIoT depicts the concept of four hierarchical layers, as mentioned below.

1. Edge devices layer
2. Core network layer
3. Cloud layer
4. Application and services layer

As per the four-layered framework, the first and foremost layer is an edge device layer, which develops the interface of MIoT devices with the patient at the remote locations, which collects the patient's parameters like ECG, blood pressure with the help of body surface bio-potential electrodes, smart wearables, or implantable biosensors [23].

The core network layer mainly deals with middleware hardware systems through wired or wireless systems and makes the smooth transfer of patients' real-time parameters to the designated locations. With the help of primary and essential technological framework, the core network layer initially acquires data and then processes it to the

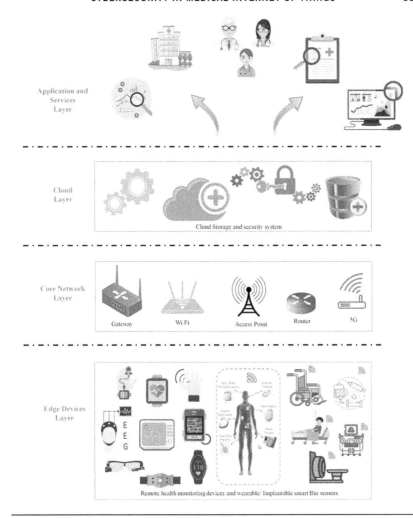

Figure 5.3 MIoT architecture.

cloud layer for storage. The cloud layer consists of the medical data storage system.

The last and topmost layer is the application and service layer. This layer facilitates the adapted and custom-made medical services and helps the end users or stakeholders to resolve their requirements regarding utilization of MIoT system. Here, the interesting fact is that the fundamental technique applied in each of these layers is different from each other. Overall, the MIoT system along with smart healthcare instruments is employed to provide a better healthcare facility to society.

Many protocols are used to improve and effective transmission of data from the four layers of MIoT architecture and to reduce power consumption for transmission of data, as well as to provide security and privacy, in MIoT service provisioning. It is important to note that each layer's protocols serve a distinct purpose. For example, data transmission protocols between MIoT sensor devices and gateways must be decided based on the MIoT application [24].

For the sake of giving readers a clear picture of the security and privacy concerns associated with the entire ubiquitous MIoT ecosystem, this section aims to provide an overview of the MIoT devices used in the previously mentioned four-layer MIoT architecture.

5.3.1 Edge Devices Layer

The medical data acquisition from the patient's body is accomplished in this layer. The physical body parameters like blood pressure, body temperature, and pulse rate can be measured by connecting respective smart instruments to the patient and real-time data is accumulated and communicated to the central medical data centre through the rest of the MIoT system [25]. Depending on the state of art, the devices used in this layer are classified as shown in Figure 5.3. Table 5.1 describes the remote health monitoring devices and wearable/implantable smart biosensors used in MIoT.

Table 5.1 MIoT Facility Monitoring Devices

CATEGORY OF MIOT DEVICES	PURPOSE AND EXAMPLES
For Patients follow-up	patients medical record and line of treatment, referring medical experts.
For visitor follow-up	authenticity and count of visitors
Hospital staff management	medical (physician, surgeon), paramedical (nurses, ward boy) and supporting (office admin) staff
Hospital assets management	tracking of oxygen cylinder, stretcher, wheelchairs
Environment monitoring	weather prediction system, pollution control
Building Automation	HVAC system, centralized air conditioning system
Security Management	CCTV, digital door locking system, ultrasonic fencing management system

5.3.2 Devices Engaged in Core Network Layer

The core network layer is accountable for content distribution and its faithful routing to the designated network without loss of data. The following devices are employed in this layer.

Wired or wireless channels: The MIoT smart devices are designed to configure wired as well as wireless communication networks to connect with the end users. Apart from this, the MIoT devices can be configured with the traditional Wi-Fi based wireless sensor network. Contrary to this, the imaging machines like MRI, CT, and X-ray machines are connected with extra high voltage cables. Most of the imaging machines are bulky and fixed at isolated location within hospital premises [26].

Radio Communication Channel: For short-distance wireless communication, radio frequency identification and detection (RFID) techniques, Bluetooth-like low-powered wireless communication channels are useful to connect with MIoT smart devices. Most of the wearable biosensors are low power Bluetooth enabled for short range and high-speed cellular communications like 3G and 4G networks are utilized for long-range wireless communication.

5.3.3 Devices Engaged in Application and Service Layer

To connect physical MIoT devices to users, an application and service layer exists. In order to provide services tailored to the needs of the stakeholders, the collected data from the edge device layer are transformed into meaningful data through the core network layer and stored in cloud or dedicated servers [27]. Rather than using dedicated servers, the cloud offers greater flexibility, convenience, and scale than does the former. This is evident in the shift of most device manufacturers to using cloud-hosted applications.

5.4 Challenges in MIOT

Connected infusion pumps and patient telemetry monitors are just two examples of how medical facilities are using MIoT technology to provide top-notch patient care. Frost and Sullivan predict that by 2023, the health sector will have 40 billion connected IoT and medical devices.

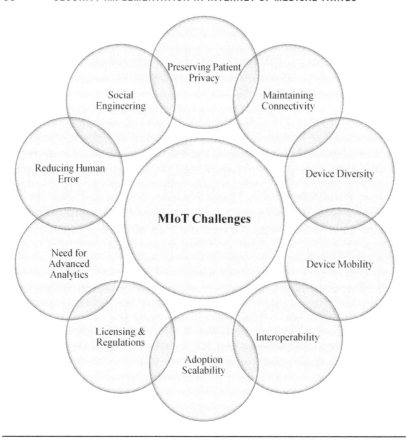

Figure 5.4 MIoT challenges.

Healthcare network administrators face unique challenges, as shown in Figure 5.4, when implementing IoT, unlike those in other industries. There are many issues to deal with, including strict privacy regulations, connectivity issues, and so on [28,29].

5.4.1 Preserving Patient Privacy

82% of healthcare organizations had significant security incidents in 2020, according to the HIMSS cybersecurity survey. What's the deal? There are averages of 15 to 20 medical equipments per hospital bed that are susceptible to attack because of their reliance on outdated technology.

If you're looking for an example, most hospitals use at least 11 MRI machines for at least 20 years before replacing them, according to GE healthcare. With reference to a recent KLAS research report, a third of all connected medical equipments are unpatched, so their manufacturer no longer supports them, making them susceptible to new vulnerabilities.

It is important to note that many of the medical devices in use today do not support security parameters necessary for today's healthcare systems and are not designed to be connected to other facilities. Thus, they are more susceptible to security breaches.

A breach of security in any industry is a serious matter, but a hospital's equipment supporting human life is particularly vulnerable. Several pacemakers and insulin pumps, for example, have been re-called by the Food and Drug Administration (FDA) due to potential security issues. If these critical devices are compromised, they could result in serious harm or even death.

Patients' safety is the top priority for health information tech-nology (HIT) professionals, who are on the front lines of this battle. IT managers should rethink their security strategies in light of their limited resources and look for new approaches to streamlining their monitoring, detection, and response to possible security threats.

When imaging systems and intravenous pumps are grouped together and monitored collectively, IT teams can more quickly identify anomalies and prevent a threat from becoming a problem before it has a chance to spread.

5.4.2 Maintaining Connectivity

Patients, doctors, and other healthcare workers should be able to rely on 100% connectivity at all times considering service in the health-care industry and the related high-risk factors. An alarming 45% of medical device connections initially fail, according to a recent study by HIT Infrastructure.

Restricted network capacity or deficiency of IT teams can all lead to the failure of these connections; these are just some examples. Those odds are simply unacceptable in a healthcare setting like a hospital. The question is: How can IT managers in the medical sector reduce latency while still ensuring connectivity [30]?

Dependable network infrastructure is the first step in ensuring continuous connectivity. In order to maintain the numerous systems and connected devices that are dependent on the network, IT teams require a flexible, adaptable, and secure network.

If the network infrastructure is not automated, it's difficult for IT teams to recognize and alleviate connectivity issues more quickly and effectively.

5.4.3 Device Diversity

This means even the purpose of devices will vary depending on the manufacturer because there are no agreed-upon standards among medical IoT product manufacturers. To put it another way, a MIoT device made by one manufacturer would not be able to connect to another made by another manufacturer, making it difficult to devise unified security schemes for the entire ecosystem.

5.4.4 Device Mobility

When used for treatment, diagnosis, or data handling, MIoT device's performance suffers significantly if it can only be stationary and located in one place. Another example is a network outage, which can have potentially life-threatening consequences if the device is unable to communicate with the outside world. This makes mobile and functional MIoT devices a priority.

To overcome the issue of device mobility the use of dual network can be one of the solutions. The performance of a device is enhanced when it is able to switch between different network configurations. It should be a safe network switch once again.

5.4.5 Interoperability

After medical data acquisition, it is processed and stored for further analysis to improve patient health outcomes; MIoT integration is beneficial. Because of its lack of interoperability, the MIoT system is often difficult to access when needed. Incorporating upgraded technologies and devices into current systems becomes more difficult. As a result, it necessitates either an expensive transformation or the creation of entirely new networks, both of which are expensive and adaptation of open platforms and open-data standards can be the solution under such situations. Different healthcare departments have little to no communication. By utilizing open data standards and secure open platforms, MIoT providers will be able to share more data, which will help to alleviate some of the interoperability issues that currently exist.

5.4.6 Adoption Scalability

A big question mark remains over whether or not the MIoT will be able to keep up with the current rate of growth and expand into more people's lives. Connected medical devices can have a significant impact on patient outcomes and healthcare costs, but not all healthcare organizations, clinicians, and patients are aware of this.

5.4.7 Licensing and Regulations

Getting a license to sell the product, integrating it into a medical facility, and looking for new markets are all on the list of MIoT challenges. The actuality is that most of the devices designed to gather, transmit, or analyze data must meet regulatory requirements and obtain appropriate licensing before they can be used and all of this may take a long time.

5.4.8 Need for Advanced Analytics

Gigabytes of data are useless unless they can be sorted, analyzed, and forecasted using effective algorithms. And it's not just about the tools that keep medical devices working and alert if something needs to be fixed; along with determining the risk of heart malfunction or an attack. It's in situations like these, the MIoT can make a real difference in people's lives.

5.4.9 Human Error Sinking

Even though healthcare facilities are more complex and reliant on technology than ever before, healthcare IT budgets and staff are not expanding at the same pace, and are even contracting. Only 28% of hospitals in the United States claim to have a fully staffed health IT workforce, as per the HIMSS Leadership and Workforce Survey, and out of that only 37% of respondents in the same study predicted an increase in IT staff in 2019. Automation of network is a hot topic these days. Consider how infusion pump technology has improved dramatically as a result of automation. Infusion pumps used to be able to download drug catalogues from a local server. A warning would be issued if a member of the medical staff altered a dosage other than the catalog's range. As of today, electronic medical records (EMRs) can be linked to next-generation infusion pumps. An automated network improves healthcare outcomes, enhances patient engagement, and streamlines the overall hospitalization process along with minimizing administrative expenses.

Using network automation, healthcare IT can standardize and streamline staff processes, enhance patient engagement, and improve healthcare outcomes. As a result, healthcare organizations will be able to spend less time on administrative tasks and more time caring for their patient.

Human talent together with technology can achieve seamless and efficient healthcare service. It is the responsibility of healthcare IT teams to bring this vision to fruition and to create amazing patient experiences in the future healthcare industry.

5.4.10 Social Engineering

As a result of the enormous way that social media has over the end users, or patients in this case, many of them are more willing than ever to share their private information publicly. Because of their large user base, cybercriminals view these sites as a new and lucrative distribution platform for malware. When it comes to these websites, end users should steer clear of giving out personal information to strangers.

5.5 Security and Privacy Issues in MIoT

The recent statistics say nearly nine out of ten healthcare organizations have reported at least one security breach involving MIoT devices. Ransomware attacks on healthcare organizations accounted for nearly half of all incidents in 2020.

Ransomware attacks using medical devices as a gateway have been reported at many healthcare organizations. In 2017, Wanna Cry

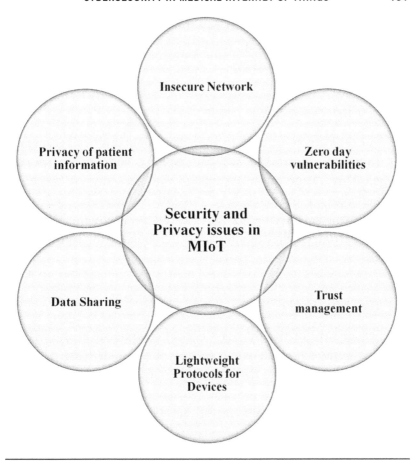

Figure 5.5 Security and privacy issues in MIoT.

was the largest ransom ware attack on medical systems with over 200,000 devices worldwide. The weak built-in security, vulnerable Windows operating system to cyber attacks, and end users' unawareness caused these ransomware attackers and hackers to look for MIoT devices that were highly susceptible to compromise. Ransomware is clearly the most common cause of healthcare data violation [31–33]. Figure 5.5 describes the security and privacy issues of MIoT.

5.5.1 Insecure Network

Complete dependency of medical IoT devices on WI-FI like a wireless network, causes the major damage to network security.

Default username and password as settings by the manufacturer may help to weaken the authentication process and becomes the main goal of network-level attackers.

5.5.2 Zero-Day Vulnerabilities

MIoT devices are vulnerable to zero-day vulnerabilities because of their inherent universality and the rapidity with which threats change. This raises questions about the necessity of frequent updating devices to patch any possible vulnerability prior to malicious attackers trying to take advantage of them. When it comes to intruders, they're always on the lookout for feeble spots or links.

5.5.3 Trust Management

The management of the trust is a critical component of the MIoT because it ensures the safety and privacy of the underlying data. In order to send and receive data, it is necessary to connect almost all devices to the Internet.

However, the massive amount of data being composed by these MIoT devices, reliable data compilation is becoming a major challenge. The trustworthiness of big data becomes a major issue in healthcare as a result of this enormous volume of data. So, to guard against security and privacy breaches, researchers are examining the difficulties of trust management. The network and application layers are hindered by these trust management issues.

5.5.4 Lightweight Protocols for Devices

Policy and proxy rules must be adhered to by low-cost sensors and software applications in order to provide services. At this time, the only way to ensure sensor security at a high level is to use expensive solutions. The MIoT system is in conflict. The future of security protection is to develop security protocols that are lightweight and adaptable to different application scenarios.

5.5.5 Data Sharing

In spite of the rapid advancement of healthcare information technology, the phenomenon of Information Island is becoming more important and serious. Devices from different manufacturers have different data standards, which makes it difficult to standardize management. However, the inevitable future trend is for heterogeneous systems in MIoT to collaborate and share information.

5.5.6 Privacy of Patient Information

There are two types of medical records: general records and sensitive records. Infectious disease information, sexual orientation, mental health, substance abuse, and identity information are all examples of sensitive data. When sensitive information like this is involved, we must ensure that it is not shared with anyone who isn't authorized, even if the data is intercepted and accessed by someone who isn't authorized. Readers should keep in mind that patient-related data security and privacy are two distinct concepts. Data security is the process of ensuring the confidentiality and integrity of data during storage and transmission.

Data privacy, on the other hand, means that information can only be accessed by those who are authorized to do so. Consequently, the booming growth and service of MIoT require both security and privacy to be taken into account.

When MIoT security and privacy are not adequate, patients' privacy could be compromised, as well as their lives. It's important for readers to understand why healthcare-related IoT is such an attractive target for intruder to attacks.

5.6 MIoT Devices Vulnerable to Attack

Confidentiality-integrity-availability (CIA) triad concerns are raised by the wide range and uniqueness of these devices. HIPAA, patient data safety, and in general information security are all affected. There have already been six medical IoT devices that are more vulnerable than others, according to recent news reports.

5.6.1 Insulin and Infusion Pumps

Around 50% of medical IoT devices presently in service are the infusion pumps and medical professionals can easily administer blood or medicinal fluids like saline solution from a distance. This helps to provide multiple infusions at a time with improved patient care and is cost effective also [34]. However, the internet-based infusion pumps with wireless remote controls weaken the technology. Referring NISTs recently released guidelines will be helpful for more understanding on how to secure wireless infusion pumps in the healthcare industry.

5.6.2 Smart Pens

Patient care documentation has never been easier, thanks to the creation of digital technology, smart devices, and touch screens, but there are new HIPAA security concerns that need to be addressed as well. Smart pens are a simple target for cyberattackers because it holds the treasure of patient's data.

5.6.3 Implantable Cardiac Devices

Implantable cardiac pacemakers and the related devices used to program them externally have been another disruptive innovation in healthcare [35]. Patients may be at risk due to security flaws in these devices, which is not a surprise. A simple DOS attack on a pacemaker has been found to be lethal, according to the researchers.

The FDA has issued four safety communications since 2017 related to implantable cardiac devices and alerted healthcare providers and stakeholders about the cybersecurity associated with Medtronic's implantable cardiac pacemakers. Medtronic reported fixing the security issues but continues to update FDA about possible vulnerabilities as safety communication.

5.6.4 Wireless Vital Monitor

Even after a patient has been discharged from the hospital, wireless devices that can transmit vital signs such as heart rate, blood sugar, and more via Bluetooth are a convenient way to keep track of their health. Mobile phones, applications, and other devices make it simple for doctors and patients to be notified when vital signs are abnormal. Wireless monitors must use encrypted networks and applications to communicate in order to prevent the data and device from being vulnerable to cyberattacks.

5.6.5 Temperature Sensors

You may have heard about the private club that was hacked by a smart thermometer in their lobby fish tank. It's funny and true at the same time: when it comes to healthcare temperature control, there are many things that are at risk than just fish.

IoT-enabled temperature systems are difficult to monitor and critical to avoid a foreseen attack, as IoT is adopted across healthcare systems. These days, the cost of sensor technology is low enough that healthcare management is eager to upgrade with the Internet of Things if they haven't already (see Figure 5.6).

5.6.6 Security Cameras

Mirai is the botnet that launched the largest-ever distributed denial of service (DDoS) attacks by connecting to other connected Internet of Things devices. One of the biggest DDoS attacks is provoked by the botnet when configured with other interconnected IoT devices should not have escaped your notice. Internet-connected devices connected to the Mirai botnet can be used to launch massive DDoS attacks against well-known services, applications, websites, or organizations using simple, default login credentials. In addition, cameras that are linked to the Internet provide entry points for patients' personal information.

5.7 Future Direction

MIoT innovations, in short, provide a cost-effective, highly efficient, and quality healthcare services and applications on time. The key specifications and scenarios that we can expect to see in MIoT security in the coming years are mentioned in literature [36–38].

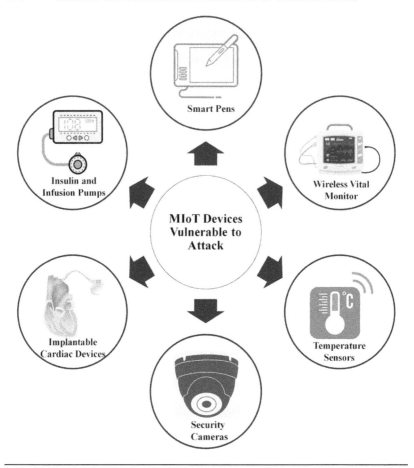

Figure 5.6   MIoT devices vulnerable to attack.

AI has made a significant impact on the IoT healthcare market in recent years, and this has aided in the development of the MIoT business.

Thus, it is clear that AI-powered solutions will play a significant role in real-time security monitoring in the future. There is no doubt that the solution for MIoT security relies on three features to effectively alleviate risks, including the detection of risks, network monitoring, and event management, where AI is a fundamental part of these solutions to offer a detailed outline and the capability of prompt responding to attacks while carrying out real-time monitoring.

Most of the MIoT devices are miniature in size and do not have sufficient computational or memory capacity, so large-scale, extremely adaptable computing and high-capacity infrastructures are required for data processing and storage. A stable cloud environment provides scope for large-scale expansion and flexibility, and becomes the first choice of any healthcare organization to deploy their application server over there. This is the focus of the security of data processing and storage, i.e., cloud environment.

Embedded security will take precedence over end-to-end security in the design of MIoT devices and components. The MIoT development process will necessitate a secure design. To ensure that healthcare organizations are more secure, security standards and regulations will be tightened.

To maintain an individual organization's position and avoid any negative security events in the future, healthcare organizations will invest rapidly in advancing the organization's information security policy. A firewall, password protection, and the ability to block unnecessary services are all common features of traditional network routers. However, modern network routers will continue to improve in terms of security and intelligence, making them a better option for securing the network's entry points.

The use of biometric identity management in healthcare facilities is on the rise. More advanced healthcare organizations and pharmaceutical companies are currently investigating this, along with multi-factor authentication.

Most of the healthcare organizations are opting for biometric applications as an additional layer of security, and it is estimated to grow this scheme in the coming three to five years. This will also improve identity monitoring and access control to be served and well-defined clinical practice healthcare organization.

5.8 Conclusion

Devices based on the Internet of Things, such as IoT-enabled MIoT, e-healthcare, and other IoT-oriented medical solutions are reshaping the healthcare industry as a whole. MIoT is gradually helping healthcare providers, including doctors, nurses, hospitals, and clinics, to provide the patients with the most effective, prognostic, and precise medication. In order to meet the ever-increasing demands of the digital society, it will be necessary to integrate IoT sensors into the existing healthcare service solutions. The four-layered architecture of MioT is presented in this chapter. Additionally, the security and privacy concerns related to MIoT sensor data and how to get rid of them are also discussed. As a result of this chapter, MIoT-based healthcare systems will benefit from new ideas.

References

1. Thilakarathne, N.N., Kagita, M.K. and Gadekallu, T.R., 2020. The role of the internet of things in health care: A systematic and comprehensive study. *Available at SSRN 3690815.*
2. Thilakarathne, N.N., 2020. Security and privacy issues in iot environment. *International Journal of Engineering and Management Research, 10,* pp. 26–29.
3. Alsubaei, F., Abuhussein, A. and Shiva, S., 2017, October. Security and privacy in the internet of medical things: Taxonomy and risk assessment. In *2017 IEEE 42nd Conference on Local Computer Networks Workshops (LCN Workshops)* (pp. 112–120). IEEE.
4. Darwish, S., Nouretdinov, I. and Wolthusen, S.D., 2017. Towards composable threat assessment for medical IoT (MIoT). *Procedia Computer Science, 113,* pp. 627–632.
5. Tarouco, L.M.R., Bertholdo, L.M., Granville, L.Z., Arbiza, L.M.R., Carbone, F., Marotta, M. and De Santanna, J.J.C., 2012, June. Internet of things in healthcare: Interoperatibility and security issues. In *2012 IEEE International Conference on Communications (ICC)* (pp. 6121–6125). IEEE.
6. Alsubaei, F., Abuhussein, A., Shandilya, V. and Shiva, S., 2019. IoMT-SAF: Internet.
7. Hossain, M., Islam, S.R., Ali, F., Kwak, K.S. and Hasan, R., 2018. An internet of things-based health prescription assistant and its security system design. *Future Generation Computer Systems, 82,* pp. 422–439.
8. Pattewar, G., Mahamuni, N., Nikam, H., Loka, O. and Patil, R., 2022. Management of IoT devices security using blockchain—A review. *Sentimental Analysis and Deep Learning,* pp. 735–743.
9. Gaikwad, S.R., Patil, R.Y. and Borse, D.G., 2019, January. Advanced security in 2LQR code generation and document authentication. In *2019 International Conference on Nascent Technologies in Engineering (ICNTE)* (pp. 1–4). IEEE.
10. Pirbhulal, S., Samuel, O.W., Wu, W., Sangaiah, A.K. and Li, G., 2019. A joint resource-aware and medical data security framework for wearable healthcare systems. *Future Generation Computer Systems, 95,* pp. 382–391.
11. Kang, J. and Adibi, S., 2015, June. A review of security protocols in mHealth wireless body area networks (WBAN). In *International Conference on Future Network Systems and Security* (pp. 61–83). Springer, Cham.

12. El-Hajj, M., Fadlallah, A., Chamoun, M. and Serhrouchni, A., 2019. A survey of internet of things (IoT) authentication schemes. *Sensors*, *19*(5), p. 1141.

13. Bhole, D., Mote, A. and Patil, R., 2016. A new security protocol using hybrid cryptography algorithms. *International Journal of Computer Sciences and Engineering*, *4*(2), pp. 18–22.

14. Almotiri, S.H., Khan, M.A. and Alghamdi, M.A., 2016, August. Mobile health (m-health) system in the context of IoT. In *2016 IEEE 4th International Conference on Future Internet of Things and Cloud Workshops (FiCloudW)* (pp. 39–42). IEEE.

15. Yogesh, P.R. and Devane, S.R., 2018, July. Primordial fingerprinting techniques from the perspective of digital forensic requirements. In *2018 9th International Conference on Computing, Communication and Networking Technologies (ICCCNT)* (pp. 1–6). IEEE.

16. Patil, R.Y. and Devane, S.R., 2019. Network forensic investigation protocol to identify true origin of cyber crime. *Journal of King Saud University-Computer and Information Sciences*.

17. Sangpetch, O. and Sangpetch, A., 2016, October. Security context framework for distributed healthcare IoT platform. In *International Conference on IoT Technologies for HealthCare* (pp. 71–76). Springer, Cham.

18. Dimitrov, D.V., 2016. Medical internet of things and big data in healthcare. *Healthcare Informatics Research*, *22*(3), pp. 156–163.

19. Li, C., Hu, X. and Zhang, L., 2017. The IoT-based heart disease monitoring system for pervasive healthcare service. *Procedia Computer Science*, *112*, pp. 2328–2334.

20. Laplante, P.A. and Laplante, N., 2016. The internet of things in healthcare: Potential applications and challenges. *It Professional*, *18*(3), pp. 2–4.

21. Dridi, A., Sassi, S. and Faiz, S., 2017, October. Towards a semantic medical internet of things. In *2017 IEEE/ACS 14th International Conference on Computer Systems and Applications (AICCSA)* (pp. 1421–1428). IEEE.

22. Deore, S., Bachche, R., Bichave, A. and Patil, R., 2021, May. Review on applications of blockchain for electronic health records systems. In *International Conference on Image Processing and Capsule Networks* (pp. 609–616). Springer, Cham.

23. Awotunde, J.B., Adeniyi, A.E., Ogundokun, R.O., Ajamu, G.J. and Adebayo, P.O., 2021. MIoT-based big data analytics architecture, opportunities and challenges for enhanced telemedicine systems. In *Enhanced Telemedicine and e-Health* (pp. 199–220). Springer, Cham.

24. Kelly, J.T., Campbell, K.L., Gong, E. and Scuffham, P., 2020. The internet of things: Impact and implications for health care delivery. *Journal of Medical Internet Research*, *22*(11), p. e20135.

25. Zeadally, S., Siddiqui, F., Baig, Z. and Ibrahim, A., 2019. Smart healthcare: Challenges and potential solutions using internet of things (IoT) and big data analytics. *PSU Research Review*.

26. Secundo, G., Shams, S.R. and Nucci, F., 2021. Digital technologies and collective intelligence for healthcare ecosystem: Optimizing internet of things adoption for pandemic management. *Journal of Business Research*, *131*, pp. 563–572.

27. Deore, S., Bachche, R., Bichave, A. and Patil, R., 2021, June. EHR-Sec: A blockchain based security system for electronic health. In *International Conference on Soft Computing and Signal Processing* (pp. 295–303). Springer, Singapore.

28. Elhoseny, M., Thilakarathne, N.N., Alghamdi, M.I., Mahendran, R.K., Gardezi, A.A., Weerasinghe, H. and Welhenge, A., 2021. Security and privacy issues in medical internet of things: Overview, countermeasures, challenges and future directions. *Sustainability*, *13*(21), p. 11645.

29. Jackson Jr, G.W. and Rahman, S.S., 2019. Exploring challenges and opportunities in cybersecurity risk and threat communications related to the medical internet of things (MIoT). *International Journal of Network Security & Its Applications (IJNSA) Vol*, *11*.

30. Patil, N. and Patil, R., 2018, January. Achieving flatness: With video captcha, location tracking, selecting the honeywords. In *2018 International Conference on Smart City and Emerging Technology (ICSCET)* (pp. 1–6). IEEE.

31. Perwej, Y., Akhtar, N., Kulshrestha, N. and Mishra, P., 2022. A methodical analysis of medical internet of things (MIoT) security and privacy in current and future trends. *Journal of Emerging Technologies and Innovative Research*, *9*(1), pp. d346–d371.

32. Alblooshi, M., Salah, K. and Alhammadi, Y., 2018, November. Blockchain-based ownership management for medical IoT (MIoT) devices. In *2018 International Conference on Innovations in Information Technology (IIT)* (pp. 151–156). IEEE.

33. Gaurav, A., Psannis, K. and Peraković, D., 2022. Security of cloud-based medical internet of things (MIoTs): A survey. *International Journal of Software Science and Computational Intelligence (IJSSCI)*, *14*(1), pp. 1–16.

34. Hei, X., Du, X., Lin, S., Lee, I. and Sokolsky, O., 2014. Patient infusion pattern based access control schemes for wireless insulin pump system. *IEEE Transactions on Parallel and Distributed Systems*, *26*(11), pp. 3108–3121.

35. Pycroft, L. and Aziz, T.Z., 2018. Security of implantable medical devices with wireless connections: The dangers of cyber-attacks. *Expert Review of Medical Devices*, *15*(6), pp. 403–406.

36. Wirth, A. and Grimes, S.L., 2020. Medical device cybersecurity—At the convergence of CE and IT. In *Clinical Engineering Handbook* (pp. 253–258). Academic Press.

37. Coventry, L. and Branley, D., 2018. Cybersecurity in healthcare: A narrative review of trends, threats and ways forward. *Maturitas*, *113*, pp. 48–52.

38. Willing, M., Dresen, C., Haverkamp, U. and Schinzel, S., 2020. Analyzing medical device connectivity and its effect on cyber security in german hospitals. *BMC Medical Informatics and Decision Making*, *20*(1), pp. 1–15.

6

Security and Privacy Aspects of AI and IoT in the Healthcare Industry

R. MALTHIYAR AND K. JHAJHARIA

Manipal University Jaipur, India

Abstract

Recently, AI and IoT are gaining more popularity because they are cost-effective and easy to use while saving a lot of time and effort. At the same time, security becomes our biggest concern. The data stored in the IoT devices are very vulnerable and can be easily leaked. Here, security plays a major role in the safety and security of data. Cyberattacks can result in life-threatening consequences. The slightest loophole in Healthcare 4.0 may lead to a healthcare data breach, where hackers can gain full access to patients' personal information. Cyberattacks are of major concern these days because of the way how our day-to-day activities have shifted from offline to more online due to COVID. In these times, the need for the healthcare industry and advanced technology has increased. With all these necessities, it is very important for the technology and healthcare sectors to go hand in hand. This will make human life easier. With these advancements, security will play an essential role as the more advancements in technology the more risk of data breaches. Hence, more optimized security models are required. In this chapter, we will study how AI is used for cybercrime and how can we use AI, IoT, and blockchain to protect the devices in the healthcare sectors.

6.1 Introduction: Background

Nowadays, we use technology in all aspects of life, whether it's education, health, or just for entertainment. Technology has become

DOI: 10.1201/9781003269168-6

one of the basic needs of our lives, part and partial of everyone's life. You cannot imagine a day without your technical devices like your cell phones or personal computers.

In today's era of tech, sectors are seen increasing all across. We also witness the emergence of health sectors at a similar pace. Presently, there are many technological advancements taking place in the health sector. For instance, magnetic resonance imaging (MRI) is used to scan various organs of the body in detail. It helps detect rather than diagnose conditions like torn ligaments or tumors. Hence, technology and healthcare industries need to go hand in hand and in unison with the upcoming market.

Over the years, the health sectors have developed a lot. With the advent of technology, they have further developed in growth and performance. The healthcare sector has been technologically revolutionized from 1.0 to 4.0. Let me pen the era of revolution in the growth in terms of technical advancement of healthcare over a period of time.

- Healthcare 1.0: Doctor's centric.
- Healthcare 2.0: It had manual and electronic healthcare records of patients. The electronic records were introduced. Therefore, we can say that the intervention of technology in healthcare had taken place from here.
- Healthcare 3.0 – It was more patient-centric.
- Healthcare 4.0 (current scenario) – Here comes the technical revolution which involves the use of artificial intelligence (AI) and the Internet of Things (IoT) [1]. This advent of technical evolution gave rise to cybercrime. This further got augmented during this pandemic time when people were glued to their devices. During this lockdown period, almost all the activities/work were done online. Students studied and attended online classes. Office goers worked from home like attending meetings, conducting meetings, and sending everything through mail. There were no personal or physical meetings like a conference room or board room meeting. This kind of scenario led to an increase in cybercrimes. According to the *Hindustan Times*, cybercrimes have increased by 11.8% in 2020 compared to those in 2019.

These statistics revealed that more involvement of technical devices increases the chances of being a victim of cybercrime. Having said that devices make our life easy and more efficient, we will not be able to perform well in the absence of these devices. Many time-taking tasks can be done within a few seconds and with accuracy. Hence, it is very clear that dependency of all of us on technology increases though there are certain drawbacks to the facility also posed to us over the period of time.

Similarly, Healthcare 4.0 has increased efficiency in diagnosing diseases. Several devices based on artificial intelligence (AI) and the Internet of Things (IoT) have made different ways of diagnosing a disease easy to use with an accurate outcome. The Internet of Things (IoT) in the medical field is known as the Internet of Medical Things (IoMT).

Since the technology and healthcare industries are advancing, it is very important to maintain the privacy of data. At present, due to the evolution in technology, it has been very easy for hackers to breach the data.

The data stored in the database of the healthcare industries are very sensitive. It contains important details of the patient such as their contact information, insurance details, and other such valuable and personal information. These confidential details can be easily misused by hackers. They can use this data to either blackmail innocent people, maybe corrupt the data or manipulate the data, or sell the data to some harmful people. If this could be the scene, then it is a havoc and people will end up facing difficulties rather than serving the purpose and making the life simple.

To tackle this problem, we need to set up strong security systems on these devices to maintain data privacy. Therefore, in order to protect and plug the gaps, we are required to find the loopholes in the given raw models, and then try to come up with a solution on how to fix these loopholes. Even the smallest loophole can prove to be very dangerous.

However, perfectly securing the devices in Healthcare 4.0 has always been a challenging task [2]. Recent technological developments have brought a revolution in the health sector for feasible transmission of patients' data. One of the prominent applications of health monitoring is the Internet of Medical Things (IoMTs). A rising trend in healthcare is the Internet of Things (IoT), which offers essential services for both patients and medical professionals in the treatment of a range of illnesses. They are used to monitor patients' data to provide necessary suggestions and services. Since patient data is so important, protecting it becomes our top focus in these applications. The present generation has seen the widespread use of biometric, machine learning, and artificial intelligence (ML/AI) systems that use authentication and anomaly detection techniques to secure medical systems. Efficiency must be taken into account in the Internet of Medical Things (IoMTs) since sensor devices have limited power and battery life. This is necessary to maintain a balance between safety and user-effective operation. Healthcare sectors are easy and beneficial prey for cybercriminals. Firstly, they can easily sell patients' treatment and payment details to the insurance companies on the darknet with fraud intention. Secondly, they can perform ransomware attacks on the database containing devices and corrupt the device leading to damage in patient's information. Lastly, like stated above, Internet of Medical Things (IoMTs) are susceptible to tampering, that is, hackers can easily have access to these devices and manipulate the data.

Hence, due to the above-mentioned issues, privacy in the healthcare sector has become a major concern for all of us. To investigate the privacy measures we need to study how hackers breach the database. The kind of software they use to get access to data. Most importantly is getting to know the kind of malicious intentions they have during these attacks.

After knowing the methods these attackers use and their intention, we need to study how we can prevent our devices from these kinds of attacks. We will study different ways to deal with different kinds of security problems. Our main goal will be to reduce the vulnerability of data. We need to increase the privacy of data and for that we need to study the different aspect of working of devices and the way it is connected through network. Therefore, we will be studying the working of Internet of things (IoT) and artificial intelligence/machine learning (AI/ML)–based devices. Thereafter, we will be discussing what can be the vulnerabilities that these devices or the newly invented models could have. Further, we will discuss how we can increase the privacy of data, and the loopholes in these devices on which we have to work.

6.1.1 AI Used for Cyber-Attacks

The study of creating machines that are capable of tasks like speech recognition, language translation, and decision-making falls under the umbrella of artificial intelligence, a subfield of computer science. Artificial intelligence is described as the simulation of human intelligence in devices that have been trained to act and think like people. With the advent of technology, innovations in the field of artificial intelligence (AI) are increasing day by day. Tech researchers are trying different aspects of artificial intelligence (AI) to make our day-to-day easy and effective. AI eases a lot of tasks, which is tedious to a normal human being.

> EXAMPLE 1: For instance, a Google assistant helps you to easily locate the things you are searching for, with just the help of your voice. It does all the work from setting up an alarm to calling someone with just one command. This is how AI has proved to be a boon to society. At the same time, as AI is advancing, people with malicious intent have started misusing it. They have started finding loopholes in these devices and trying to breach the data. They try to steal personal information and tend to blackmail the users.
> EXAMPLE 2: For example, a Keylogger is a software that when installed in a device tracks all the keystrokes done by the user. All the keystrokes are stored in a file that can be accessed by a remote user. This is so dangerous as all the passwords, or any other important and confidential details entered by the device's owner are being tracked by some other person. This person who has some malevolent intentions can misuse this information, which can be life-threatening for the other person.

This is only one way explained above through which a hacker can get into the system. Moreover, Keylogger is one of the easiest ways to breach data. There are several other ways through which the attacker can get into a particular system. One very common attack is a malware attack; that is, an attack through viruses, trojans, ransomware, and so on. Here, the attacker takes hold of the system or the application and kind of corrupts it. Here, either the network denies access to the system or the attacker retrieves the data of the victim or disrupts the whole system.

Denial of service (DoS) attacks are also very common these days. In this attack, the attacker sends several network packets with traffic that overloads the system, hence damaging it. The advanced version of DoS attacks is distributed denial of service (DDoS) attacks. This attack aims to capture as many systems as it can. The difference between DDoS and DoS attacks is that a DoS attack is only for a single system while a DDoS aims for multiple systems. This can disrupt the whole organization.

There are many such attacks, and the list is endless. The other attacks that can be taken into consideration are SQL injections, man in the middle attacks, phishing, and so on. There have been so many applications developed for such attacks. Moreover, these applications are easily available on the Internet to download. These kinds of attacks steal the freedom of the users to explore and experiment with their creativity on technical platforms. You need to be careful while using any kind of application or software as you never know what you have downloaded may contain viruses [3].

Poisoning AI systems is alarmingly easy. Since AI is still in its development stage, it has been very easy for the attackers to get access to systems and harm the system. They try to manipulate the data in such a way that the AI models give wrong outputs. The attacker who is unsuccessful in breaching the data tries to tamper with the inputs given in by the user so that proper identification rather than the training of the model becomes difficult. It can be done very easily while staying anonymous; that is, no one will come to know who is trying to harm the system. Attackers try to reverse engineer the whole model to observe the whole workings of the model. Therefore, we can see how AI is being weaponized for the dubious intentions of hackers.

Cybercriminals employ AI with the scale and effectiveness of their social engineering attacks. As stated above, they can easily get into any system and manipulate the behavior of the whole model.

Cybersecurity attacks are not the same as they used to be a decade ago. They have changed a lot. We should say that even the attacks have evolved with the dawn of technology. Cybercriminals are very intelligent. They try to find out new ways and develop new AI models to breach into other systems. Today, cyberattacks have become a worldwide problem. It is really life-threatening to innocent users. The way attackers manipulate the data, it has become really unsafe for users to work online.

Especially during these pandemic times, when everything went to an online mode, the risk in privacy increased a lot. There was a drastic increase in cyberattacks in 2020 compared to yesteryears. People got into a lot of trouble because attackers had hacked the systems that contained their important and confidential details, such as their account details or some passwords.

Also due to the pandemic, the burden on the healthcare sector had increased. It had to provide all the necessary services like proper medicines and care to the patients in the hospital on time. Any kind of carelessness could have led to a huge casualty that actually happened. Citizens of India have seen a huge loss in the last wave of COVID, which was the delta phase. Many families lost their loved ones in that pandemic.

In these kinds of scenarios, privacy and security of data in the healthcare sector play a major role. Even a small carelessness in the security of the data could lead to life-threatening results. The AI- and IoMT-based devices are susceptible to attackers. They will try to breach the data and maybe manipulate the data or gather some information and try to blackmail the patient. Both kinds of attacks can prove to be life-threatening for patients as they can lead to some kind of mistreatment or wrong diagnosis.

Hence, it is really important to study various ways that an attack can be done on the devices. Here, AI plays a major role as a dangerous weapon in such attacks.

With the use of AI, attackers can conveniently locate vents to enter a network without protection. This means that the attack can take place in a very short period. AI is so vulnerable that it finds loopholes very easily, which is difficult for human beings to even detect. A bot can easily use data from previous cyber-attacks to identify the changes in the security in these AI- and IoT-based models.

The healthcare sector is a common target for cyber attackers. In fact, it is the most targeted sector globally. According to www.bmj.com, it has been seen that 81% of healthcare organizations claim that they do not have a strong cyber defense to protect their data. This clearly shows that the patients' data is prey for attackers. Since healthcare industries are easy to attack, therefore it is targeted the most.

The year 2020 has been cruel for many people worldwide. All thanks to the COVID for making the year 2020 the worst year for many of us. Also, 2020 has seen some of the major cyberattacks. These are the worst cyberattacks in history. These kinds of attacks in the healthcare sector left the world baffled.

One such event that can be discussed is the Blackbaud attack. Blackbaud is the world's leading cloud software company. It provides all kinds of technical services like cloud software and data intelligence systems for education and healthcare institutions.

> EXAMPLE 3: In 2020, there was a ransomware attack on a Blackbaud system that was connected to a healthcare organization. The attacker breached the system containing over 10 million patients' data. Although the security team was able to stop the attack, still the attacker had already received many patients' details such as name, contact, and so on. This kind of attack can be life-threatening as you never know what the attacker is trying to do with such a large set of data. Maybe he would call up the patients with a fake identity and try to harm them in a certain way or sell the patient's health history to the insurance companies on the darknet.

> EXAMPLE 4: Another example of such a life-threatening attack that shook the whole world was the Magellan Health attack. Magellan Health is a care company that manages the most complex areas of healthcare sectors and comes up with solutions to solve problems faced in these sectors. This cyberattack was done in the month of April 2020. It was also a ransomware attack. It was a severe attack wherein 3.65 lakh patients and employees were harmed. The hackers impersonated themselves as Megan Health client and started interacting with the people who worked in the company. Moreover, all this was done 5 days before the attack. This technique is called social engineering phishing in which the attacker interacts with people and tries to gather all the information about its target systems. All the information like patients' contact details, insurance details, and other confidential details were breached by the attackers. Attackers had access to the system's database.

There were many such destructive attacks that were noticed in 2020 like Health Share of Oregon and Aspenoite. Moreover, in all these attacks, ransomware attacks have played a prominent role. It had made it easy for the attackers to gain access to the systems containing large databases. Ransomware attacks are those attacks in which the attacker installs software in the target system and encrypts all the data, making it inaccessible to the user. Then the attacker demands some ransom from the user in order to bring the data back to its normal phase. In this attack, the attacker has already gotten access to the database, leading to any kind of manipulation in the data.

From the above cyberattack cases, we can see how dangerous these attacks are. These attacks can disrupt anyone's life within seconds. And this is not done to harm only one or two people, but millions of people at a time. These attackers can spoil millions of lives within seconds.

These kinds of hackers who hack systems with malicious intentions are known as Black Hat Hackers. These hackers always try to breach systems with threatful intentions. These attackers mainly work with terrorist organizations. Their main aim is to break into systems and steal important information like passwords and other confidential information and harm the system and its owner. Also, if their goal is not achieved, then they will make sure to corrupt rather than destroy the whole system so that they would not get caught.

Hence, we need to observe all kinds of cyberattacks that take place in order to strengthen security. We need to look after each loophole in the networks connected to the newly invented AI and IoMT devices, especially in the healthcare sector. As stated above, healthcare organizations are easy prey for attackers because they contain all the important information about patients that can easily be misused. Moreover, at the height this information can be so conveniently misused that you would not even notice, and the attacker's goal has been achieved. It will be too late when you will know what exactly happened and it would be very difficult to find out who did it.

While the healthcare sector continues to offer life-saving services and is undoubtedly a blessing for all of us, the number of cyberattacks in this industry raises concerns about its weak security. It is high time now that this is taken note of and to come up with solutions to put a halt to these attacks. These solutions should be highly defensive and difficult for hackers to break into the system.

6.1.2 AI Used as a Defense against These Cyberattacks

In the previous paragraphs, we have seen how these Black Hat hackers are using AI against us. The kind of applications they have developed in order to breach the data are very dangerous. We have observed several techniques of corrupting the systems. Now it's time for a counterattack. We need to find efficient solutions for such attacks and protect those newly invented devices. We need to strengthen AI in such a way that it can be used against such malicious attacks.

As mentioned above, there is much research going on in the field of AI to make our day-to-day lives easy and more efficient. One of the topics of research is the privacy and protection of data in our systems.

There are many applications invented to detect viruses or other malware in the system, such as Quick Heal and McAfee. They have an inbuilt model that automatically detects the malware and warns the user against it. It also has a feature in which it can automatically remove the malware-containing data and ensure the system is safe.

A rat race has emerged in technological advancement. Artificial intelligence (AI) is quickly assuming a central role in the global power struggle to dominate the race in emerging technologies and the battlefield of future warfare [4].

AI and IoT have gained a lot of popularity. There are so many new inventions every day. It has literally become a competition among all the countries worldwide to become the world's technology hub.

Machine learning (ML) and artificial intelligence (AI) are high in demand these days. It is due to the increase in computing power, data collection, and storage capabilities. Along with these improvements in AI, such as self-driving cars, language translators, and big data, there is also a rise in cyber threats such as botnets, malware, and phishing.

Machine learning (ML) and artificial intelligence (AI) have taken a boom in society. Every other gadget contains an AI model working in the background. Moreover, researchers are attracted to this field because it has the capability to work and analyze complex datasets.

Especially in the healthcare sectors, the Internet of Medical Things (IoMTs) and artificial intelligence (AI)–based models are daily used.

Nowadays, people cannot imagine technology without AI. Our daily lives are dependent on these automated models.

In the healthcare industry, doctors are helpless without AI- and IoMT-based diagnoses. CT scans, MRIs, X-rays, and many other systems are based on IoMT and AI. In fact, they are basic but a very good example of IoT-AIS (Internet of Things with artificial intelligence systems). Today, researchers are also working on the IoT-AIS concept [5]. They are trying to bring a revolution to the whole world and are trying to connect the physical world to the digital world.

These days, the metaverse is a hot topic to discuss. It is trying to unite the physical reality into the virtual reality. Imagine consulting your doctor in a virtual reality platform, that is, in 3D (three dimensions) without even stepping out of your house. It will be so convenient, especially for senior citizens or specially abled citizens.

This is how technology is advancing. However, with this advent, it becomes our responsibility to be aware of the strength of the security in these kinds of models. This is because you need to store all kinds of data, like your personal details, in them to test their workings or use it for your own benefit. But, after observing several cyberattacks in history, the security of these newly invented devices has a big question mark on it. The inventions in the areas of AI and IoT really excite us, but have we never thought of their security or tried to build any AI models to increase the security.

It is high time that we must realize that our safety is in our hands. We need to investigate each detail of whatever new applications are being developed. The European Union Directive 2002/58/EC establishes security and confidentiality norms and regulations that must be followed to protect patient information in electronic healthcare systems from unauthorized parties [6]. We need something impactful that acts as a counterattack for these Black Hat Hackers. Moreover, the first sector that needs to be focused on is the healthcare sector, because it contains sensitive information about people that can be misused. Hence, there is a strong need for AI to be weaponized.

Researchers are working on the security framework of the devices to protect the data. They are using various cryptographic techniques in the framework to strengthen the security of the system. But still, that seems ineffective after those major cyberattacks have been observed.

This shows that we need to work more effectively on improving the security of the systems [7].

One of the ways through which we can combat these attacks is through an ML-based framework that uses an electrocardiogram (ECG) signal in a security framework. The robustness of ECG-based bio-keys against false attacks is one of the primary advantages of employing them. One of the challenges faced for ECG setup is that it needs high entropy to ensure resistance against attacks. High entropy and stability at the same are quite a task to do [8].

In such cases, instead of ECG, we can use our traditional quantization methods. In these methods, the problem is addressed by mapping noisy illustrations into a distinct vector followed by applying hash functions. But these days hackers are familiar with the quantization methods because it has general characteristics. Hackers have enough parameters and resources to get access to those systems that are protected using quantization methods. The end results after having access to the systems are known to all [9].

Hence, we need to integrate the ML model with our current security frameworks to develop reliable health monitoring systems.

We can also use CNNs (convolution neural networks) [10]. It basically covers four layers rather four branches of neural networks. A CNN is known to predict the accuracy of the given AI model. We can use this feature to test the accuracy of the security model that is built. The four layers are very helpful in detecting the speed and accuracy of the model. By applying CNN in the security, the accuracy increases by 20% from the actual accuracy rate. The four branches increase the width of the CNN and decrease the parameters, which helps in increasing the efficiency of the whole model.

We can even try updating the data; that is, replacing the old data with new data so that hackers would not compromise with the old data for their own good. Data should be encrypted from time to time and its key should be distributed only among the authorized authorities, ensuring they are not involved in any malicious acts.

From the above-mentioned cyberattacks, we have seen that social engineering played a major role in executing the attack. Social engineering is a way in which the hackers interact with the organization's authorities and try to gain some confidential information.

Hence, organizations especially related to healthcare must be extra careful in trusting people with the encryption key of the systems.

As discussed in the above article, a keylogger is a common software that can be inserted into a system that will provide the attacker with all the keystroke information. Hence, to prevent that, we can build an AI model that can easily locate a keylogger installed in the system and alert the user regarding the same.

Also, from the cyberattacks seen for a decade in the healthcare sectors, ransomware attacks are very common. Attackers insert malware into the system and when they get access to the database, they ask for heavy ransom. Although there is software like Quick Heal and McAfee to locate such malware still, we need a strong model to detect malware in the system. Also, that software must be capable of taking action on time if someone is trying to harm your system or network. AI systems are being trained to recognize patterns, detect malware, and recognize even the smallest details of malware or ransomware attacks before they enter the system. In fact, today, network frameworks should be built in such a way that if someone tries breaching data through a denial of service (DoS) attack then it should immediately alert the user and take automated action.

Also, as discussed earlier, social engineering attacks are also very common. For that, we can develop an AI/ML model that detects the intentions of a person. Basically, it will detect the intentions of a person through its pulse rate of scanning the retina of the eye. In addition, we can include an MRI feature that reads the behavior of a person's brain and detect the intention. This whole new model is a mix of the Internet of Things (IoT), artificial intelligence (AI), and machine learning (ML).

There is a lot of potential in the field of ML and AI that would help in strengthening the security framework of a system. Information security is purely based on the CIA triad. CIA stands for confidentiality, integrity, and availability. There are many other AI frameworks that have been proposed in order to increase the security of the network in the healthcare sector.

> EXAMPLE 2: For example, eDiag. It is an AI/ML framework that helps in preserving and maintaining the privacy of data. It will use the concept of a non-linear support vector machine (SVM). In the e-healthcare sector, SVM is used commonly but still, there are many healthcare organizations that do not even know about this concept.

One more framework of AI/ML that can be proposed is Health-Guard. It will detect any malicious activity that is being done in the smart healthcare systems. It is using the concept of artificial neural networks (ANNs), decision trees (DTs), random forest (RF), and K-nearest neighbor. This will alert the user against any malicious threat in the system and take necessary actions. We can also use the support vector machine (SVM) concept in mobile applications to keep patients' data private and safe.

While breaching the system, the attacker has to face an approximately 0.3% strong security framework. While using an AI-based security framework, the strength increases to as high as 15%; that is, the attacker has to face a 15% strong security framework. This is the strength we need in our systems. The security should be so high that it becomes highly difficult for attackers to breach it.

According to a survey, it is said that around 56% of healthcare institutions have said that there is a high need to secure the systems with the help of AI-based security frameworks. Hence, there is a strong urge to come out with such security frameworks that are efficient and work very well against Black Hat Hackers.

We can also develop an AI-based software that will scan the whole model of the given system and identify the breach risks. It will give details of every loophole in the system that needs to be mended and also gives a solution to how they can be mended.

In recent years, AI has evolved into a vital tool for improving the work of human information security teams. Since humans can no longer scale to adequately protect the dynamic business attack surface, AI offers much-needed analysis and threat identification that can be leveraged by cybersecurity specialists to reduce breach risk and boost security posture. AI is capable of categorizing hazards, swiftly identifying malware on a network, managing incident response, and seeing incursions before they occur in terms of security.

AI is increasingly turning into a necessary tool for enhancing the efficiency of IT security teams. Humans can no longer scale to effectively protect an enterprise-level attack surface, as was previously mentioned. Security professionals may reduce breach risk and improve security posture using AI's analysis and threat identification. Additionally, AI can direct incident response, find and prioritize hazards, and detect malware attacks before they happen. Therefore, despite any potential drawbacks, AI will advance cybersecurity and assist enterprises in developing stronger security postures.

AI is the new emerging technology in today's era. Researchers are trying to shift every physical work to digital work. They trying to digitalize everything and make human life easy. Hence, with this emerging technology, it is important to keep the data safe and confidential. Therefore, we need to focus more on system security than on new inventions.

Having said that, if the security strength is high, and we have complex network connections and encryptions that are difficult for an attacker to decrypt so that we can freely enjoy the lavishness of the new innovations, we need not fear data breaching and stealing confidential information.

6.2 Security in IoT Devices

Wireless technologies, micro-electromechanical systems, micro-services, and the Internet have all come together to form the Internet of Things (IoT) [11]. Healthcare, facility management, agriculture, energy, and transportation are just a few of the industries that use IoT solutions. The IoT transition is being driven by numerous enterprises. Interconnected networks are starting to include IoT devices including wearables, commercial appliances, connected electronics, smart grids, and intelligent cars. The networks collect, process, log, and store a significant amount of data produced by these devices.

Today, all your data, location, email accounts, financial information, and pictures reside on your smart devices or IoT devices, which is a treasure trove of data for hackers. With the increase in selling and buying of IoT devices in the market, they are now outnumbering people. The number of IoT devices is expected to reach 75 billion in 2025.

The IoT has introduced a range of new technologies with associated capabilities into our daily lives. As the IoT is an evolving technology, the immaturity of technologies and services provided by various vendors will have a broad impact on organizations, leading to complex security issues. IoT security is difficult to ensure as the devices use simple processors and stripped-down operating systems that may not support sophisticated security approaches. Organizations using these devices as part of their network need to protect both the devices and the information from attackers.

As industrial companies are digitizing their industrial facilities to enhance operational efficiency through Internet connectivity and remote data access, they need to increasingly focus on cybersecurity to mitigate new threats and safety issues arising from the convergence of operational technology and information technology. Organizations need to understand the landscape of cyber threats, industrial infrastructure, and business. Before implementing cybersecurity policies and controls, organizations need to identify and prioritize key risks and threats that will have the greatest impact on their business. IoT technology includes four primary systems: IoT devices, gateway systems, data storage systems using cloud technology, and remote control using mobile apps. These systems together make communication between two endpoints possible [12].

1. Sensing Technology: The gadgets' inbuilt sensors collect data on a number of environmental factors, such as temperature, gases, location, the operation of some industrial machines, or patient health information.
2. IoT Gateways: Gateways are used to connect and communicate between an IoT device (internal network) and the end user (external network) by bridging the gap between them. The gateway transmits the data gathered by the IoT device's sensors to the connected user or cloud.
3. Cloud Server/Data Storage: The acquired data passes via the gateway and then arrives in the cloud, where it is stored and subjected to data analysis. The user receives the processed data and can then act in accordance with the knowledge gained.
4. Remote Control Using Mobile App: The end user may monitor, control, get data from, and perform particular actions on IoT devices from a distance using remote controllers such as mobile phones, tablets, laptops, and other devices equipped with mobile apps.

IoT technology is growing so quickly that it has become ubiquitous. With numerous applications and features but a lack of basic security policies, IoT devices are currently easy prey for hackers. In addition, upgrades to IoT devices have introduced new security flaws that can be easily exploited by hackers. To overcome this significant issue, manufacturing companies should consider security as the top priority, starting with planning and design, and up to deployment, implementation, management, and maintenance.

Owing to the significant growth of the paradigm of the IoT, an increasing number of devices are entering our lives every day. From the automation of homes to healthcare applications, the IoT is everywhere. We cannot undervalue the risk of cyberattacks, even though IoT devices have the potential to make our lives simpler and more comfortable. IoT devices are vulnerable to numerous cyberattacks because they lack fundamental protection.

The Internet of Things (IoT) idea has recently become more popular in the healthcare industry. This is due to its affordability, illness management system, improved medicine management, and remote data monitoring. At the same time, a significant concern is its security. Gadgets in the healthcare and life science industries include surgical instruments, telemedicine, wearable devices, health monitoring devices including implanted cardiac pacemakers, ECG, and EKG. The Internet of Medical Things, or IoMT, is easy pickings for hackers [13].

In order to access the user's device and data without authorization, hackers target IoT devices. An army of hacked IoT devices may be exploited by hackers to create botnets, which are then utilized to execute a DDoS assault.

The data stored in IoMTs is a lucrative target for Black Hat Hackers. This is because IoT is still emerging, and research is going on. Therefore, right now its security framework is at a very basic level.

Potential vulnerabilities in the IoMT system can result in major problems for organizations. Most IoMT devices come with security issues such as the absence of a proper authentication mechanism or the use of default credentials, absence of a lock-out mechanism, absence of a strong encryption scheme, absence of proper key management systems, and improper physical security.

Healthcare data security is an important feature of the Health Insurance Portability and Accountability Act (HIPAA) Rules [14]. According to this Act, 10,000 people are targeted by breaching healthcare systems every day.

The kind of attacks that happen in healthcare sectors are:

- Signal Jamming Attack: Electromagnetic interference or interdiction using the same frequency-band wireless systems.
- Access Control: Gaining physical or remote access to the device.
- Denial of Service (DoS) Attack: Making service unavailable for legitimate users by flooding the system with communication requests.
- Eavesdropping: Collecting exchanged messages.
- Sinkhole Attack: Compromised nodes try to attract traffic by advertising a fake route.
- Sybil Attack: The reputation system is subverted by forging multiple identities.
- Bluesnarfing Attack: Gaining illegal access to Bluetooth devices to retrieve information.
- ZED (ZigBee End-Device) Sabotage Attack: Damages the ZED by sending a signal periodically to wake up the object to drain its battery.
- MITM Attack: Listening to the communication between two endpoints.

Discussed below are some of the challenges facing IoT devices that make them vulnerable to threats, especially in healthcare sectors due to which the above-mentioned kind of attacks occur [15]:

- Lack of Security and Privacy: The majority of IoT devices used in the healthcare sector today are online and hold sensitive information. Even the most fundamental privacy and security standards are lacking on these devices, which hackers might use for nefarious purposes.
- Vulnerable Web Interfaces: A lot of Internet of Things (IoMT) devices include embedded web server technology, which leaves them open to assaults.
- Legal, Regulatory, and Rights Issue: Certain security concerns are brought up by the connectivity of IoMT devices, however there are no rules in place to address these concerns.
- Default, Weak, and Hardcoded Credentials: The authentication systems on IoMT devices are among the most often

targeted targets for cyberattacks. These devices typically ship with weak and default credentials, which a hacker might use to access the devices without authorization.

- Clear Text Protocols and Unnecessary Open Ports: IoMT devices frequently employ protocols that transfer data in clear text and with open ports since they lack encryption mechanisms for data delivery.

- Coding Errors (Buffer Overflow): The majority of IoMT devices available today contain embedded web services that may be used in the same ways as web service platforms. Therefore, changing such functionality could result in problems with technological infrastructure such buffer overflows, SQL injection, etc.

- Storage Issues: IoMT devices typically have less data storage, but the amount of data they can gather and transmit is unbounded. As a result, problems with data management, storage, and protection arise.

- Difficult-to-Update Firmware and OS: While updating firmware is a crucial step in addressing vulnerabilities in a device, its functionality may be compromised. Because of this, product creators or manufacturers could be reluctant or outright refuse to offer product assistance or make improvements while their goods are still in the development stage.

- Interoperability Standard Issues: The interoperability problem, which is essential to the sustainability and long-term expansion of the whole IoMT ecosystem, is one of the largest challenges for IoMT devices. Manufacturers' inability to test application programming interfaces (APIs) utilizing standard procedures and mechanisms, their inability to secure devices using third-party software, and their inability to manage and monitor devices using a standard layer are all problems brought on by the lack of interoperability in IoMT devices.

- Physical Theft and Tampering: IoMT devices can be physically attacked by being tampered with, having malicious programs or data injected into them to make them function the way the attacker wants, or by having their hardware modified. When the gadgets are not adequately protected physically, counterfeiting might potentially be a problem.

- Lack of Vendor Support for Fixing Vulnerabilities: Vendors are reluctant or typically unwilling to grant other parties access to their devices, despite the fact that updating the firmware of the devices is necessary to safeguard them against specific vulnerabilities.
- Emerging Economy and Development Issues: The prospects for IoMT devices to be used widely across all industries have added levels of complexity for legislators. The new environment these devices have created gives lawmakers another perspective as they create new guidelines and regulations for IoMT devices.
- Handling of Unstructured Data: The volume, pace, and variety of unstructured data will expand along with the number of linked devices, which will make handling it more difficult. It is crucial for enterprises to comprehend and identify the data that is useful and actionable.

If MISCONFIGURED and MISAPPREHENDED, the IoT poses an unprecedented risk to personal data, privacy, and safety. If APPREHENDED and PROTECTED, IoT can boost transmissions, communications, delivery of services, and standard of living.

The threats to the Internet of Medical Things (IoMT) can be sorted into three primary categories: security, privacy, and safety. As they all concern the same equipment and its connectivity, these categories are all interconnected. Since IoT devices will have access to the most private or sensitive personal data, including health records, financial information, and Social Security numbers, they will quickly become more widespread in our lives than cell phones [16].

If these three categories of threats are prioritized and several required techniques are employed to overcome these issues, it will result in enhanced and secure communication between two endpoints, fewer cyberattacks on devices, and a better user experience; in addition, it will also result in cost savings and efficiency gains.

Seeing the vulnerability of the IoMT devices towards the attackers it has become really important for all of us to develop a strong security framework to keep the healthcare data safe and secured. There are many ways through which we can prevent IoMT hacking. We can implement end-to-end encryption in those devices. It is very important to disable telnet that is port 23. Locate control system networks and devices behind firewalls and isolate them from the business network [17]. Regularly, monitor traffic on port 48101, as infected devices attempt to spread the malicious file using port 48101. Position of mobile nodes should be verified with the aim of referring one physical node with one vehicle identity only, which means one vehicle cannot have two or more identities. Create an asset inventory for mapping the network and for discovering all paths of ingress and egress to determine whether the IoT network has its own Internet gateway that does not follow the security policies or applicable laws, regulations, and contracts. Implement a secure boot option that uses cryptographic code-signing techniques, and ensure the device executes code generated by the device's original equipment manufacturer (OEM) [18].

To design secure and protected IoT devices, security issues should be properly considered. One of the most important considerations is the development of a secure IoT framework for building the device. Ideally, a framework should be designed in a way that provides default security, so that the developers do not have to consider it later.

6.3 Blockchain Technology Protecting Data

Blockchain technology is in a lot of discussions nowadays. It is one of the emerging technologies in today's era. Organizations need to use blockchain to protect their data. Blockchain technology is advancing rapidly these days. Blockchain has proved to be one of the efficient ways to secure data.

It's based on principles of cryptography, decentralization, and consensus, which ensure trust in transactions. The advantage of blockchain is that the data cannot be changed by a single user.

Blockchain provides a most important feature that is end-to-end encryption. As mentioned above, the healthcare devices based on IoMT and AI/ML need a strong security framework and end-to-end encryption is one of the important features that must be added. Due to this feature, the communication between the user and the authorities will be safe from hackers because the messages have been encrypted.

Blockchain helps in applying CIA Triad in real-life security frameworks. CIA stands for confidentiality, integrity, and availability. Confidentiality means that all the data is confidential and only the respective organizations' authorities can access them. This is really important, especially in the healthcare sectors, because the patients' data is very sensitive and critical.

Integrity is ensuring that the data has not been manipulated and is intact. This is basically trusting the organization with your personal information. People especially in healthcare sectors trust the authorities and provide them all their personal information. Now it is the organization's responsibility to keep those data safe and intact. Availability means data remains available only to specific people. Also, only the limited amount of data remains available. Nowadays, hackers can easily access the database. In blockchain, the data is available through different nodes in that particular network. Hence, hackers easily get into nodes and manipulate the data.

However, blockchain provides a very secure platform. The way it is connected to different nodes in its security framework, the strength of the security becomes very strong. In this framework, distributed denial of service (DDoS) attacks is very difficult. Hackers cannot use this method to get into the system as the connectivity with nodes in blockchain makes the security strong.

In blockchain, the whole system is decentralized such that all the data is available to all the nodes of the framework, and everything is encrypted. The decryption is done in a specific way that is known only to the authorities [19].

Earlier, blockchain was used only for cryptocurrency, but now it is also used for security purposes. This is because it keeps all the records of transactions and databases safe and secure. Hence these days it is even being used for security purposes. Blockchain provides a direct interaction between the authorities and the users. There is no third party in between, hence making the system really secure to use. Blockchain technology has become really important in the healthcare sector as the data stored in their system is very crucial. The data in these systems are very sensitive and hence need strong protection measures. As technology is advancing, blockchain seems to be the most efficient way to secure data in today's era. Although no one can claim that the data is 100% secure, but still blockchain seems most efficient.

According to www.builtin.com, around 176 million patients' data were exposed to a breach from the year 2009 to 2017. The hackers stole banking information and some important information regarding patient's treatment. Blockchain is transparent as well as private. It keeps the patient's data safe, which maintains the individuality of the patient. In this way, the patients can share their details with the doctors or healthcare providers quickly and in a secured manner.

There are many companies that provide blockchain technology in healthcare applications.

    EXAMPLE 1: For instance, Akiri is a company that works specifically in developing useful applications for healthcare sectors. It basically uses the concept of big data in order to build new applications. This company uses blockchain in order to keep the patients' data safe and secure. They ensure that the patient can share their data with the healthcare authorities quickly, safely, and in an organized manner. With this technology, the patient need not worry about any data breach or any kind of tampering with their personal information. The Akiri system is a network and protocol that sets policies and configures data layers while instantly confirming the sources and destinations of data. It does not store any data of any sort.

    EXAMPLE 2: Another example that we can take up is BurstIQ. It is a Colorado-based company. This company is mainly known for its usage of big data and cybersecurity in its healthcare software. This platform helps patients to securely share their personal information with the authorities. Its blockchain technology helps them to securely store and share patients' information with correct authorities also has a license saying that it strictly follows Health Insurance Portability and Accountability Act (HIPAA) rules. Since it provides up-to-date information about patients it can also help root out abuse of opioids or other prescription drugs.

There are many such companies that use blockchain technology in protecting their healthcare applications or software. Some other companies like Factom, MedicalChain, and so on use blockchain in order to secure their healthcare applications from Black Hat Hackers.

The healthcare data comprises the electronic healthcare records (EHRs). It consists of all the personal details of the patients like their contact information, health reports, and so on. Hence, it is very necessary to protect these data and according to today's advent, blockchain seems the most reliable source of security.

To sum up, we can state that this is a very serious matter though very convenient while carrying a couple of loopholes that need to be plugged in to make it more effective and useful for the end user. It is very important to treat these loopholes, or else it can create a disaster for society, especially in the healthcare sectors where the details must be confidential. There are very high chances of these data to be manipulated as they are very easy to be hacked. Even though we are advancing in technology, the security will always remain a major concern, especially in Internet of things (IoT) and artificial intelligence (AI)–based technologies.

As mentioned above, the technology in the healthcare sector is advancing at a rapid pace. To combat this fast pace, we need to take extra care of its security.

Even though security is advancing, there are many places where the data has been handled manually and there is not much use of technology. According to a survey, around 50% of the hospitals do not think that there is any need of technology to manage data of their hospitals. Many of them do not even know that technology has been this advanced. Hence, first of all we need to make these organizations aware of the different technologies available to make their work efficient.

Further, the researchers have to work mainly on security of the newly invented devices. As discussed, there are several ways in which we can protect IoMT/AI-based devices. Also, we have seen the kind of attacks the hackers use; ransomware attacks are very common these days. There is a high need to weaponize AI against these malicious hackers, else they will breach data and misuse them which will harm us.

Hence, technology has a lot of advantages while it carries its own disadvantages along with it. Therefore, using the same judiciously and effectively can bring wonder in one's life.

References

[1] Chen, C., Loh, E.-W., Kuo, K.N., and Tam, K.-W., 2019. The Times They Are a-Changin' – Healthcare 4.0 Is Coming! *Journal of Medical Systems*, 44(2), 40.

[2] Hathaliya, J.J. and Tanwar, S., 2020. An Exhaustive Survey on Security and Privacy Issues in Healthcare 4.0. *Computer Communications*, 153, 311–335.

[3] Zouave, E., Gustafsson, T., Bruce, M., and Colde, K., n.d. Artificially Intelligent Cyberattacks, 50.

[4] Pandya, J., 2022. The Weaponization of Artificial Intelligence [Online]. *Forbes*. Available from: https://www.forbes.com/sites/cognitiveworld/2019/01/14/the-weaponization-of-artificial-intelligence/ [Accessed 14 Mar 2022].

[5] Ghazal, T.M., 2021. Internet of Things with Artificial Intelligence for Health Care Security. *Arabian Journal for Science and Engineering*.

[6] Radley-Gardner, O., Beale, H., and Zimmermann, R., eds., 2016. *Fundamental Texts on European Private Law*. Hart Publishing.

[7] Gopalan, S.S., Raza, A., and Almobaideen, W., 2021. IoT Security in Healthcare Using AI: A Survey. In: *2020 International Conference on Communications, Signal Processing, and their Applications (ICCSPA)*. Presented at the 2020 International Conference on Communications, Signal Processing, and their Applications (ICCSPA), Sharjah, United Arab Emirates: IEEE, 1–6.

[8] Moosavi, S.R., Nigussie, E., Levorato, M., Virtanen, S., and Isoaho, J., 2018. Performance Analysis of End-to-End Security Schemes in Healthcare IoT. *Procedia Computer Science*, 130, 432–439.

[9] Pirbhulal, S., Pombo, N., Felizardo, V., Garcia, N., Sodhro, A.H., and Mukhopadhyay, S.C., 2019. Towards Machine Learning Enabled Security Framework for IoT-based Healthcare. In: *2019 13th International Conference on Sensing Technology (ICST)*. Presented at the 2019 13th International Conference on Sensing Technology (ICST), Sydney, Australia: IEEE, 1–6.

[10] Xu, L., Zhou, X., Tao, Y., Liu, L., Yu, X., and Kumar, N., 2022. Intelligent Security Performance Prediction for IoT-Enabled Healthcare Networks Using an Improved CNN. *IEEE Transactions on Industrial Informatics*, 18(3), 2063–2074.

[11] Gills, S.A., 2022. What is IoT (Internet of Things) and How Does it Work? - Definition from TechTarget.com [online]. *IoT Agenda*. Available from: https://internetofthingsagenda.techtarget.com/definition/Internet-of-Things-IoT [Accessed 14 Mar 2022].

[12] Condry, M.W. and Nelson, C.B., 2016. Using Smart Edge IoT Devices for Safer, Rapid Response with Industry IoT Control Operations. *Proceedings of the IEEE*, 104(5), 938–946.

[13] Dias, D. and Paulo Silva Cunha, J., 2018. Wearable Health Devices—Vital Sign Monitoring, Systems and Technologies. *Sensors (Basel, Switzerland)*, 18(8), 2414.

[14] Mercy Kiruba, W. and Vijayalakshmi, M., 2018. Implementation and Analysis of Data Security in a Real Time IoT Based Healthcare Application. In: *2018 2nd International Conference on Trends in Electronics and Informatics (ICOEI)*. Presented at the 2018 2nd International Conference on Trends in Electronics and Informatics (ICOEI), Tirunelveli: IEEE, 1460–1465.

[15] Elhoseny, M., Thilakarathne, N.N., Alghamdi, M.I., Mahendran, R.K., Gardezi, A.A., Weerasinghe, H., and Welhenge, A., 2021. Security and Privacy Issues in Medical Internet of Things: Overview, Countermeasures, Challenges and Future Directions. *Sustainability*, 13(21), 11645.

[16] Amaraweera, S.P. and Halgamuge, M.N., 2019. Internet of Things in the Healthcare Sector: Overview of Security and Privacy Issues. In: Z. Mahmood, ed. *Security, Privacy and Trust in the IoT Environment*. Cham: Springer International Publishing, 153–179.

[17] Bradley, C., El-Tawab, S., and Heydari, M.H., 2018. Security Analysis of an IoT System Used for Indoor Localization in Healthcare Facilities. In: *2018 Systems and Information Engineering Design Symposium (SIEDS)*. Presented at the 2018 Systems and Information Engineering Design Symposium (SIEDS), Charlottesville, VA: IEEE, 147–152.

[18] DCMS_Mapping_of_IoT__Security_Recommendations_Guidance_ and_Standards_to_CoP_Oct_2018.pdf.

[19] Singh, P. and Singh, N., 2020. Blockchain with IoT and AI: A Review of Agriculture and Healthcare. *International Journal of Applied Evolutionary Computation*, 11(4), 13–27.

7

SECURITY AND PRIVACY CONCERNS IN SMART HEALTHCARE

SUMIT KUMAR AND PRACHI AHLAWAT

*Department of Computer Science &
Engineering, The NorthCap
University, Gurugram, India*

Abstract

In today's era of digital transformation, the management of online data is becoming more critical. A seismic transition is happening in the healthcare sector from conventional, paper-based record-keeping to storing health records over electronic databases. This is going to cause a lot of problems. Consider, for instance, the privacy concern during the handover of patients' sensitive data from one healthcare provider to another. The end users must be mindful of the privacy and security consequences posed by these healthcare monitoring systems. When users give access to potentially insecure or suspicious third-party applications, they become susceptible to possible malicious attacks. With the growing usage of IoT and cloud-based technology in the healthcare domain, networking and computing technologies are now integrated into these e-healthcare services. These smart-linked devices can endanger system security and individual privacy by creating more collaborative channels. In this chapter, a wealth of ideas are presented to researchers related to IoT and cloud-based smart healthcare systems about all the potential angles relating to the security and privacy of normal users. This study pays special attention to the benefits, advantages, and difficulties inherent in the deployment of these systems in an interconnected environment.

DOI: 10.1201/9781003269168-7

7.1 Introduction

The concept of smart healthcare [1] as given by Solanas et al. [2] is that "smart-healthcare" refers to "integration of context-aware networking and sensing technologies in smart cities." Eysenbach [3] further clarified smart healthcare as a multi-tier industry that is a combination of the Internet, connectivity, and healthcare and is especially beneficial to both consumers and stakeholders. A smart healthcare system (SHS) can give healthcare providers "opportunities to deploy technologies with minimized risks and improved context awareness, by using cloud services, sophisticated sensors, networks, and data collection techniques" [4]. SHS technology is capable of monitoring, interpreting, and processing healthcare information whenever and wherever it is needed. E-health (an acronym for electronic healthcare) is a developing field that intersects with many other fields of medical informatics, public health, and which supports and drives the advancement of emerging healthcare technologies to address long-standing challenges, bring down costs, and enhance the patients' overall experience. Elderly people, for instance, can benefit from healthcare facilities in the safety of their own homes [5]. Medical data centers help authorized persons gather and pass their physiological data to doctors so that they can analyze and determine when to exchange that data with physicians for diagnosis [6]. To offer another example, a person who has diabetes collapses in their office. Many times, during this medical scene, hospital staff orders his/her past health records. Now it is much easier to figure out which health problems you may have with the aid of a smartphone application that monitors food, exercise, sleep, and blood sugar levels regularly.

To incorporate electronic healthcare, services, and overall smart healthcare programs efficiently and securely, security systems must be efficient and robust. Because of the ubiquity of IoT technologies, a large amount of research and development work has been performed on secure IoT technology, including a broad variety of IoT and cloud architectures concerning health networks [7]. Emerging disruptive technology such as the Internet of Things (IoT) and cloud infrastructure are capable of complementing their abilities when implemented as adaptable, scalable, and effective smart healthcare networks.

In contrast to traditional networking technologies, the combination of both IoT and cloud offers benefits such as ease of deployment, improved information security during transmission of data, easy access to saved records, and energy savings. Further enhancements in healthcare services can be done with the continuous innovation in IoT and cloud technology and its implementation in smart healthcare systems. This allows improved connectivity between patients, doctors, and service providers, which serves as the basis for a revolution in the healthcare industry.

System protection and privacy must be held together in order to preserve consumers' and stakeholders' trust. WHOs guidelines on ethical standards of health-related research with human experimentation classifies medical health records as personally identified, identifiable, and nonidentifiable. Based on this principle, policies that limit data collection and dissemination may be formulated, taking into account the security categories and circumstantial details of health records. In order to protect the patient's secrecy, the Medical Council of India's Code of Ethics Regulations stipulates that physicians or doctors shall not reveal patients' secret information except in the case of a court order, or where there is a serious and recognizable danger to a person or society. Administrators, physicians, and the public information officer all have a responsibility to keep the patient's personal information confidential. Researchers must also protect the secrecy of their study, related to health and other personal information, notably when the provision of confidentiality is provided in an informed consent agreement.

Three protocols are proposed by O'Keefe and Connolly [8] for securing access and usage of healthcare data: (1) having permission from the users for accessing data; (2) securing proper authentication by meeting the criteria specified for specific information, and (3) obfuscating personal information for a secondary purpose, such as activities related to public healthcare research [9]. Moreover, wireless sensor devices such as smart wearables and sensors are embedded into our everyday lives, raising unparalleled challenges with regards to security and privacy. It is also likely that these innovations are at risk of being targeted by adversaries because of their architecture. This data breach may have devastating effects both for the consumers it impacts and the company's profile. We use social (healthcare) and technological elements of smart healthcare applications to recognize protection and privacy issues, which allows us to exchange this knowledge with other researchers in similar fields.

The key contribution of this report is to define the privacy and security problems affecting smart healthcare systems and to provide an understanding of the precise methods or interventions that can be applied to deter or minimize adversarial attacks. The methodical study outlined in this chapter should serve as a reference for prospective researchers as they introduce and apply specific solutions for IoT in healthcare issues, as determined by healthcare professionals who adhere to the suggested methods and mechanisms. The remainder of this chapter is structured into the following parts to help you to develop an understanding of these problems and possible solutions: In section 7.1.1 authors explored some niche smart healthcare technologies. Based on that, we present some innovative smart healthcare concepts in section 7.1.2 and show how the integration of IoT and cloud computing plays around with smart healthcare systems. In section 7.2, they explored some existing smart healthcare security frameworks followed by the discussion on security and privacy concerns in greater detail under section 7.3. The researchers further propose some solutions to the challenges posed by these smart healthcare systems under section 7.4 and finally review and discuss open research issues for future work in this direction.

7.1.1 Existing Smart Healthcare Technologies

Smart city infrastructures have significantly helped residents by offering more comfort. With wireless sensor networks, common in transportation, healthcare, and metering, being more common, wireless sensor networks have shown up in various other implementations such as smart transportation systems, smart meters for tracking electricity/gas usage, and mobile networks for remote healthcare systems. When considering both of them, they can be used to aid in the development of Internet of Things (IoT) applications. In simple terms, the primary goal of IoT is to link all kinds of things (embedded sensors/micro- controllers/wearable devices, etc.), which allow people to have a more favorable and convenient lifestyle. According to previous ventures, including Smart Santander, IoT technology had a great effect on Smart Santander. By using sensors in numerous cities, a testbed was built to keep track of traffic patterns and assist drivers in finding parking spaces on short notice [10]. Different kinds of data can be acquired by smart city systems, and these different kinds of data can be used to improve the programs of the city government and benefit the residents. One of the advantages of the Oyster Card scheme in London is that it will produce around 7 million data records per day and close to 160 million records every month. Owing to the number of various databases being calculated in both quantity and scale, large-scale data collection systems may be used to help with the development of smart city applications, from calculating, manipulating, and evaluating a wide range of datasets.

The latest projection displayed in Figure 7.1 reflects the smart healthcare (SHS or e-health) study as being the outcome of using an e-health system as a layer above a smart city system, as discussed by Solanas et al. [2]. For the context of this example, one can suggest that both smart healthcare (s-health) can be defined as subsets of e-health, but, from the viewpoint of infrastructure, e-health will not be just about mobile devices and apps but also includes sensors and microcontrollers. As a consequence, with the use of big data analytic techniques (for example, predictive analytics, pattern recognition to name a few), an e-healthcare system can be supported by automated services, as discussed by Provost et al. [11]. A second s-health

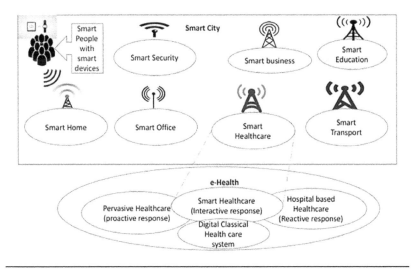

Figure 7.1   Layered diagram for smart healthcare systems [2].

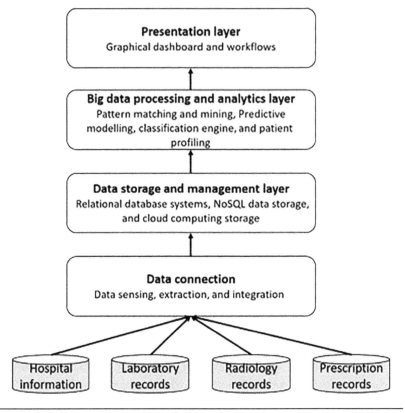

Figure 7.2 Smart healthcare system architecture [12].

platform was developed to apply several computational techniques on a broad range of health-related datasets [12].

Figure 7.2 provides a layered, modular smart healthcare structure in which the four functional layers are extended to the different types of data that will need to be linked, processed, evaluated, and displayed. If the different dataset types have been collected, the first issue to solve is the aggregation of disparate datasets (such as hospital documents, laboratory reports, radiology records, and prescriptions from pharmacies). At the link layer, modeling-related semantic ontologies can be leveraged to help form and sustain semantic communication. To achieve consistency and the ability to handle a wide variety of data sources, at the storage layer, you can use cloud-based services like relational database systems and/or NoSQL storage resources to handle organized, semi-structured, and unstructured data. Additionally, the analytic layer is capable of performing a number of different tasks

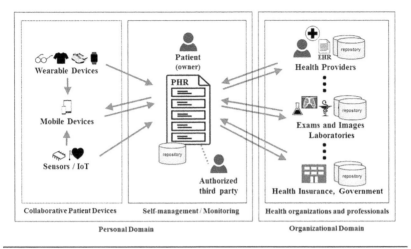

Figure 7.3 Distributed Personal Health Record (PHR) system architecture [13].

depending on the data processing specifications. When it comes to creating a user-friendly dashboard to show analytics data, an organization should aim to create a user-friendly presentation layer. Any phase of the recovery process helps physicians and experts to make more relevant and up-to-date choices.

A significant number of people have embraced healthcare data-driven systems such as HealthVault and Google Fit for their e-health services. In Figure 7.3, we see how a high-level architecture, as with the intelligent personal health record (PHR) structure [13], is suitable for building on top of. By way of HealthVault APIs, programs based outside of the enterprise can be implemented on the community-level data that is collected from across the entire population. In this way, a lightweight intelligent PHR device may be developed without the use of local storage. Another important idea underpinning this strategy is that patients have the ability to maintain and monitor their own records, and so they are empowered to effectively engage in their own care. In addition, the current PHR scheme embraces diverse methodological technologies, such as measuring techniques that are not currently used in science. For instance, as a result of tracking patient outcomes, retrieving hospitalization and testing reports, and using medical decisions, healthcare professionals may have the potential to efficiently use limited resources, while public health researchers can be predictive and defend against adverse events among a much broader population by having access to clinical and laboratory evidence in the medical history of PHRs.

To maximize the effectiveness of wireless sensor technologies, Catarinucci et al. [14] developed an IoT-aware security framework by expanding healthcare facilities and integrating them into an IoT network. Three components must be added into this architecture: A sensor network made with wireless sensors for data collection; a smart IoT gateway that enables authentication and control for the local and remote users before confidential information can be accessed; and a user interface that lets the monitoring of data, as well as a display of real-time performance. An IoT-enabled device can capture and transmit patients' real-time condition and environmental situations, as well as intelligent inferences, to a transmitting center, such as one that utilizes data with algorithms and enables the transmission of emergency alerts.

Baig and Gholamhosseini [15] classify the e-health systems according to the type of sensor being used, which are then divided into three categories as wearable health monitoring system (WHMS), mobile health monitoring system (MHMS), and remote health monitoring system (RHMS). Specifically, the WHMS requires the use of wearable devices, while the MHMS includes the use of mobile devices.

An RHMS can be developed by incorporating mobile contact and wearable tracking technologies and using it to relay critical notifications, for instance sending a critical health update to the patient's house. As can be seen in Figure 7.4, wireless body area networks (WBANs) are capable of providing patient's health-related information such as heart rate, blood pressure, ECG, and oxygen level in blood by providing sensor devices mounted on the human body.

The use of mobile devices empowers people to transfer data relevant to their well-being to the cloud systems and e-health servers for data analytics [17]. The last layer offers care to people who are farther away from treatment centers. The electronic health reports (EHRs) saved in the e-health registry will be distributed to remote hospitals.

Remote access to patient knowledge aids emergency services in addition to healthcare [18]. Sahi et al. [19] developed a multidomain structure that covers several separate classes of customers, such as doctors, pharmacists, and healthcare companies based at remote organizations. A smart access approach is developed by the connection

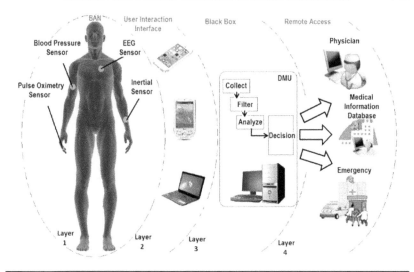

Figure 7.4 Wireless body area network architecture for smart healthcare systems [16].

of several networks, and communication technologies are implemented to shape these systems. Often known as using innovative tools to track the patients' health conditions, smart health management programs also go by the moniker of "smart use of technology." In view of the derived behavioral models from smart surveillance systems, Baig and Gholamhosseini [15] developed a generalized smart healthcare architecture, as well as a connectivity architecture for designing a smart city framework. As seen in Figure 7.5, this system can be adopted at a number of places such as the house, the hospital, and outdoors. The credibility of the patient data and its security must be protected because PHI contains particularly sensitive attributes. Based on a comprehensive analysis of current studies, two major aspects are contained in the s-health frameworks: the use of sensing technology (for example, electronic, wearable sensors) in pervasive contexts, and the use of complex data processing (such as data aggregation and deep learning methods) on heterogeneous datasets. As a result, additional security measures are required for smart health infrastructures that require the integration of a diverse array of system functionalities.

7.1.2 Innovative Smart Healthcare Concepts

Healthcare is being transformed by revolutionary smart healthcare systems, which empower users as new platforms, applications, and

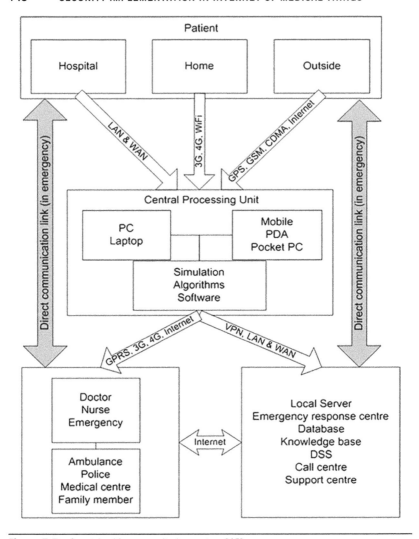

Figure 7.5 Smart healthcare monitoring system [15].

devices that were not available in the past have seen tremendous growth. Innovative e-Health solutions are difficult to distinguish because new ideas/theories are increasingly being developed and will ultimately become the new basis for digital healthcare systems, as Ambarkar and Sheokar [20] describe.

According to the investigation, the results show that protection is given to healthcare IoT systems by means of researching different architectures, which is accompanied by a debate on the future smart healthcare systems' enhancement. Benefits are presented in a recent study performed by Farahani et al. [21], in which smart healthcare developments enhance a range of applications, such as diagnostics. By integrating IoT devices, doctors would gain access to data that will help them formulate data-driven care decisions, which can increase the patient's chances of success significantly.

Abouelmehdi et al. [22] used big data to improve e-Health services, such as the exploration of information, aspects, and personal health management. In their evaluation, the delegates from the different healthcare and medical sectors claimed that IoT-based e-Health platforms provide tremendous promise for a range of areas within the healthcare field, including e-benefits health and pitfalls with respect to privacy and protection technology. Similar to Connor et al. [23], who addressed the usefulness of IoT within the smart health market, researchers in this area have discovered that privacy issues can be integrated with IoT-enabled smart healthcare. The people who are proposing the introduction of IoT to healthcare provide a realistic approach to the issues they outline. In their academic paper, Tanwar and Hathaliya [24] performed an extensive study of the literature on healthcare privacy and security problems in Healthcare 4.0. They performed an in-depth analysis of the privacy and security problems within Healthcare 4.0 using blockchain technology. And to demonstrate the benefits of protection and privacy strategies, they explored different healthcare management methods, frameworks, and tools. Related to this, Aceto et al. [25] launched Business 4.0 and clarified how Healthcare 4.0 would benefit from it. They showed examples of how Healthcare 4.0 applications may be developed, and how Healthcare 4.0 implementation of Business 4.0 technology may support them. The key aims are to provide the major benefits, such as medical care, technologies, and procedures, and medical knowledge.

A list of basic principles in the study of smart healthcare services is presented below:

- Ambient Assisted Living (AAL): For example, people living in assisted living settings could have equipment built into their surroundings, which assist them to live more independently. These systems additionally capture archive and evaluate patient behavior in order to provide remote monitors with the capacity to respond rapidly to possible emergencies and investigate reports of violence [20].

- Internet of Healthcare Things (IoHT): The healthcare industry is using integrated mobile and cloud technology features to capture real-time patient data via smart devices. We have instant access to our gathered data, which is then processed to identify and treat patients easily and effectively. To the end, though, these kinds of networks are also susceptible to security and privacy issues, which several security researchers have attempted to resolve [26,27].
- Smart Wearable Devices: IoT devices such as smartwatches, wristbands, headgears, shirts, hats, necklaces, and eyeglasses along with embedded sensors and microcontrollers are considered a particular form of smart devices. More than 90% of these systems use the IEEE 802.11 standard frequency [28,29].
- Sleep Trackers: Having sleep metrics by tracking the sleep habits of someone over the course of a night is referred to as sleep monitoring [30]. Both roles are fulfilled by these. On one hand, there is the task of formulating an analytical perception of the consistency of a person's sleep; on the other, there is a separate task of investigating the general patterns of sleep. While multiple measures can be taken to determine the quality of sleep, such as respiratory rate and body movements, only a small amount of these measurements are used for sleep monitoring in an entire sleeping session. Market sleep monitoring systems are usually not meant for systematic diagnosis of sleep disturbances. However, with technical advances in hardware and software, as well as greater usability, as well as greater affordability, the public can use them for therapeutic purposes. The following products are samples of numerous health and wellness trackers: Emfit QS, Fitbit, Withings, Beautyrest, Sleepace Reston, and Juvo. A few examples of current bed-based sleep trackers are shown in Figure 7.6.
- Blockchain-enabled devices: Over the last decade, blockchain technology has taken the world by surprise, and it is drawing interest from various industries, such as banking, government,

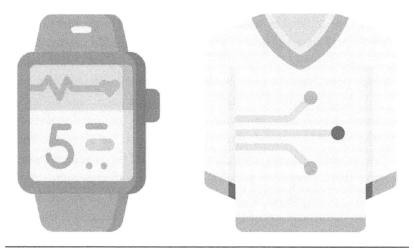

Figure 7.6   An illustration of some wearable sleep trackers [33], icons made by Freepik [34].

electricity, healthcare, and much more [31]. We have several new blockchain-based healthcare technologies, including data sources, blockchain infrastructure, healthcare implementations, and stakeholders, and they can be categorized into various levels of abstractions. According to Gordon and Catalini [32], who published a study on healthcare blockchain, they accepted that blockchain technology would allow patient-centric management of healthcare data exchange while still enforcing centralized control. In their research, they studied how blockchain technology facilitates digital access privileges, patient authentication across the network, and processing a vast amount of healthcare data. As Ray et al. demonstrate, the usage of blockchain technologies in healthcare enables increased transparency among patients and doctors, efficient collaboration between healthcare networks, and resistance to failure and data isolation due to the transparent and distributed design [31]. The proposed consensus algorithms and networks on the Internet of Things–based e-healthcare show how the core technologies of the IoT and blockchain together can be used to improve healthcare systems, they explained how these tools could be successfully harnessed. On the other hand, blockchains are very vulnerable to attack, as their simplicity makes them readily recognizable.

On the issue of flexible smart healthcare system implementations, IoT and cloud-based e-healthcare systems are highly customizable and can be designed to suit the requirements of individual smart healthcare providers. As a result, these have many different forms of IoT and cloud computing systems that provide such capabilities as continuous surveillance, proactive maintenance, patient satisfaction feedback, and AI-powered diagnostics. Both of the given facilities represent possible privacy leaks, and they should be considered when enforcing privacy security policies within a specified system. With increasing knowledge of one's privacy rights, end users are more concerned about the security of their medical records. A prime illustration of this will be a patient who has an embarrassing health problem and who has their sensitive details leaked or published to social media. As a result, it will be hard to re-establish their confidence in the health care provider, let alone near-impossible for the provider to address the problem raised by Nazir et al. [35]. They have used the Internet of Things (IoT) in healthcare by integrating mobile networking technologies and applied a rigorous literature review approach and presented practical proof on how mobile computing can support IoT solutions in smart healthcare. By leveraging the Internet of Things (IoT) in the healthcare industry, patients can benefit from privacy and protection in their medical equipment. Similar to this report, the analysis approach of Semantha et al. [36] research by a comprehensive literature review to define contemporary healthcare systems that rely on privacy by design. From there, they find out what vulnerabilities occur in the healthcare section and how to cope with them. They claim that their ideas are appropriate for the future course of healthcare research and development. Wu et al. [37] created a model, extended to social networks where users can use it via an IoT app to assist with diagnosis and self-care.

This model is capable of changing the control variable, which offers the most effective options for hospitals. Research undertaken by Khatoon et al. [38] examined how the IoT could be used in healthcare. Connecting the Internet of Things (IoT) to healthcare systems will improve efficiency and consistency for patients. In healthcare, the Internet of Things entails sensor-based smart devices that can provide accurate data for analysis and then take appropriate action.

7.1.3 Integration of IoT and Cloud Computing with Smart Healthcare Systems

Cloud computing and the Internet of Things (IoT) are innovative inventions that complement each other and have the ability to transform the way the world works. When it comes to combining IoT with cloud computing, it is referred to as the Cloud of Things (CoT) [39]. The Internet of Things includes numerous intelligently linked person, computer, device, entity, system, and application components interacting with one another using the Internet. Cloud computing and the Internet of Things (IoT) technology integrated into smart healthcare systems improves patient experiences by automated health diagnostics and therapies and offers convenience and cost reduction without compromising privacy. The convergence of IoT and cloud computing platforms for smart healthcare systems is useful since customers can access any and all of these systems and resources they need through the cloud at any time, any location, and in any environment. There are various benefits of this purchase, including protection and privacy threats that are often ignored in order to achieve ease and efficiency. The distinguishing characteristics of each IoT device are its distinct existence, its main functionality, and its basic uses. These attributes of each IoT device gather private data. Cloud computing uses Internet of Things (IoT) devices to access data and connect it to the cloud. Cloud servers in smart healthcare networks act as the middleman to handle and store the data. It makes use of the cloud, which makes authentication fast and reliable for authenticated users, who can then use this secure access to the data from anywhere.

By way of the use of innovative approaches, Kang et al. [40] set forth a brand new IoT-based methodology and system to work with technologies like mobile wellness, cloud computing, big data, and smart automation systems. Their efforts to save bandwidth and battery power by lowering the hearing threshold resulted in data integrity of up to 99%. Wang et al. [41] explored how the technical advancements in IoT devices and cloud computing can be implemented. The quantification of their system has proven that it reduces data retrieval time and resources as opposed to the current approach. The overall goal of Yamin [42] is to provide a summary of the critical value of IoT-based systems and their advantages to healthcare, particularly when it relates to data management. To gather data from different organizations, we can use big data through the Internet. Meri and Mohammed [43] used emerging innovations in healthcare to illustrate a new trend. instead, it allows people to keep closer track of their own health history, which thus improves the quality of healthcare. They presented a detailed description of IoT technology in healthcare: It is likely to be a new technology with the potential to communicate through smart devices or connected objects with different functionality such as machine-to-machine (M2M), human-to-human (H2H), and human-to-machine (H2M).

The integration of IoT-based technologies and cloud infra-structure in e-Health systems needs an extra layer of concern with regard to confidentiality, anonymity, reliability, and trust [43] as it uses network technology to link devices together. These network connections can be categorized as object-to-object (O2O), device-to-machine (D2M), machine-to-machine (M2M), patient-to-doctor (P2D), and patient-to- machine (P2M). Cha et al. [44] aimed to make connectivity and communication to IoT device resources and software simpler and showed the security shortcomings of IoT architecture. They reviewed emerging protection and privacy risks and the technologies required to address them. In a paper titled "Secure IoT: Alternative Protection and Privacy Properties to protect IoT-enabled Systems with Cloud Computing," Zhou et al. [45] addressed privacy and security characteristics, such as authentication against illegal data access, confidentiality, and anonymity to spoofing attacks, which they describe as protecting IoT-enabled systems with the help of cloud computing. Without these characteristics and properties, it is virtually impossible to preserve the privacy and security of users in IoT-enabled e-Healthcare systems.

7.2 Security and Privacy in Smart Healthcare

In this section, we offer a broad overview of technical framework specifications for smart healthcare applications, which include iden-tification, authentication, and authorization.

Systems may be developed that reduce the possibility of an intrusion as well as the risk of private data leakage. There are different kinds of protection, ranging from information privacy to personal privacy.

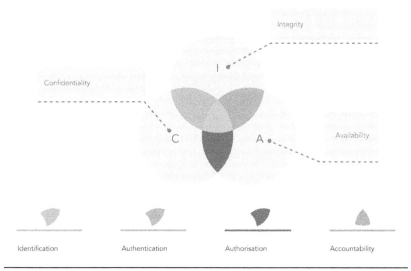

Figure 7.7 CIA triad and security goals.

Lupton's study states there are threats involved with data collection: "Sources of these risks include Internet of Things (IoT) systems that are monitoring and tracking devices' content, sending the data across the network, and, finally, in the cloud where the data is processed for review." This section includes an overview of security and privacy requirements in smart healthcare systems.

The CIA model, a theoretical framework for IT systems, has been commonly used to protect cloud-based database systems (Cherdantseva & Hilton) [46]. See Figure 7.7, where the CIA Protection Concept discusses the conditions of secrecy, honesty, and availability in terms of specifying measures to discourage improper data access; protecting data from unwanted modification; and making it accessible for dependable access and usage. Most approaches are based on guidelines that act as blueprints. Encryption algorithms are also used to guarantee security, ensuring that encrypted communications are impenetrable to attackers who do not have access to the decryption keys, "editing" rights are only open to people who have managerial positions.

Smart healthcare devices help us achieve higher productivity and thereby change our lives by monitoring our physical movements. They do, though, have a high propensity for vulnerability and privacy flaws. Using the vulnerable third-party software allows the future adversary permission to access the device remotely, which ensures that e-Health system users will become prey to malware. Subsequently, consumers use smart healthcare products in their private locations, such as their houses, deliberately or unintentionally. The machines are sufficiently safe to be infiltrated. IoT-enabled smart e-Health devices and tracking systems typically connect over the open public networks. Over the contact path, the attacker will carry out numerous attacks such as Botnet, denial of service (DoS), and man in the middle (MITM) attacks as the data are being transmitted to the server. The foregoing points are not to be ignored, since the adversary will obtain access to the data contained in the cloud by infecting it with malicious software. When the computer or storage has been accessed, an intruder has access to confidential personal data, such as private location, login credentials like username, and password. Such a data breach could severely harm the user's credibility. The illustration below (Figure 7.8) shows an IoT system implemented in a medical environment and how

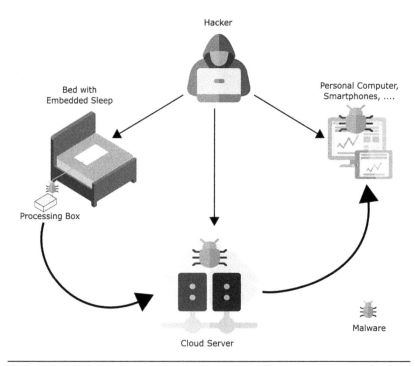

Figure 7.8   Illustration of a smart sleep-tracking pad and this serves as an explanation of how an attacker can manipulate various stages of data collection, i.e., from data extraction to end users [48].

attackers can manipulate the different phases of data collection, for example, data collection, through to end users [47].

7.2.1 Security Requirements in Smart Healthcare Systems

It is important that e-Health applications are able to be applied and employed because the implementation of smart healthcare–based e-Health systems necessitates multiple security functions such as data privacy, data integrity, confidentiality, authentication, encryption, and access transparency.

The findings of an analysis performed on the security and protection against privacy leaks in IoT-based applications by Srinivas et al. [26] found that the risks of individual data being leaked could be minimized by using a database that offers authentication and identification services.

In order to ensure the privacy of smart healthcare platforms used for smart engineering, technological creation, ecosystem simulations, and numerous educational applications, related research has centered on authentication design, with emphasis on improved security measures. Additionally, Kalyani and Chaudhari [49] devised an effective method for enhancing security in IoT-enabled systems with the use of an optimal authentication key.

It enhances the authentication security in IoT via encryption-based techniques to secure IoT-sensitive data by using highly reliable homo-morphic encoding. The key authentication and optimum key will be selected using a phase fire optimization algorithm in order to choose the optimum key for encryption. The system proposed by Yu et al. [50] offers safe authentication and a central IoT-based cloud storage solution. Companies that deal with cloud infrastructure and IoT-based solutions would have more efficient and functional resources. In order to enforce effective access control, authentication, and secure communication in the IoT-based cloud storage systems, it is important to maintain the confidentiality of the information. Additionally, ensuring security, data privacy, integrity, robustness, and self-maintenance in wireless IoT often requires a commitment to data protection and confidentiality. The usefulness of data in the IoT is critical because it presents a considerable risk to hackers seeking to leverage the opportunity offered. Researchers at the Jimenez Lab at

San Diego State University, along with other researchers, have developed new approaches for tracking and treating patients with wireless body area networks (WBAN) IoT technology. While the implementation of the new technology does come with many challenges, efficiency and security are two critical areas to solve. When you understand the broad range of applications for WBAN, it is possible that WBAN may be worn or implanted beneath the skin to serve its purpose.

Generally, smart healthcare–based applications can be tested for protection by incorporating current security and privacy analysis approaches, such as the CIA triad among others. This literature review summarizes these mechanisms as follows:

- Confidentiality is an essential factor for safe communications between a sender and receiver. To maintain the confidentiality of the entire contact network, from different IoT devices to cloud storage to smart healthcare systems, everything ought to be safe [51].
- In order to prevent any misuse of the information, data integrity guarantees that both the sender and recipient are secured from any unauthorized users. A non-repudiation check can be conducted at each node that is involved in the communication between the sender and recipient in an IoT-cloud-based smart healthcare system.
- The availability of e-Health systems means that attackers or unauthorized users are unable to disrupt or impair connectivity or service provided by the system's communication network, which is built on an IoT-cloud architecture.
- A successful access management scheme limits user access to classified information and regulates or restricts such access by assessment, judgment, and compliance.

7.2.2 Privacy Requirements in Smart Healthcare Systems

It is imperative that patients' safety be addressed across the entire data life cycle. Additionally, which individuals or departments inside the company have permission to access personal or financial records is determined by the company's privacy policy. Data privacy and security are defined as the mechanisms that are enforced to ensure that sensitive data is protected from unwanted or unintentional use, modification, or dissemination. Data security can be achieved through different approaches, including cloud storage, data anonymization, and big data processing. The privacy and security mechanisms provided by each healthcare provider can be customized to the individual needs of their users, as each healthcare system provider delivers a multitude of different programs, like continuous surveillance, preventive diagnosis, patient feedback, and AI-driven diagnostics. Wong and Mulligan [52] discussed the value of design in the light of privacy through the design, opening up lines of investigation for researchers and practitioners.

Customers have become increasingly aware of and worried about the security of their medical records. Suppose someone who suffers from a chronic illness was their personal details exposed on social media. Now consider what will happen with the individual accessing the social media, then that service would be out of the question for continued trust, and it would be an incredible struggle for that provider to regain the lost trust. Since smart healthcare–based e-Health solutions are based on the cloud, privacy is much more important. In order for smart devices to work efficiently, their users must have confidence in both the devices and the underlying technology, since that's how users capture, tag, handle and maintain their data. Privacy can be secured by maintaining sufficient oversight of user access, the use of strict protocols and checklists, and the incorporation of additional privacy regulations.

To improve the trust, anonymity, and protection of smart healthcare–based e-Health applications, the following elements should be incorporated into the core framework.

- Data life cycle safety includes authentication mechanisms that are important to maintaining privacy over the entire lifecycle of the data. This means that all the records are stored safely and then, at the completion of the process, they are deleted securely. The life cycle management of information requires both better data life cycle management as well as efficient data life cycle management to avoid information archiving, transportation, and deletion [53].

- The software's full functionality is dedicated to accommodating all legitimate interests and objectives, obviating the need for privacy and security trade-offs. It is definitely necessary and important to safeguard both security and privacy aspects without compromising the services provided.
- Proactive interventions distinguish themselves from reactive actions in that they anticipate and mitigate threats to sensitive personal data before they occur. The goal is to avoid privacy-related threats from arising instead of responding to incidents after they occur.
- Owing to the major advantages provided by big data networks, it is now important to provide location information while processing data. In order to avoid the loss, leakage, or exposure of location data relating to individual users, successful privacy policies are needed.
- The definition of privacy requires ensuring that sensitive data are secured regardless of whether or not conditions require. Since this is the case, even though someone keeps their sensitive details to themselves, their privacy is not compromised. As such, it should be recognized that no effort on the part of the user is taken to protect their privacy, as this is incorporated into the mechanism by nature. Contrasting with conventional systems, which need active human interaction to modify and secure records, the new approach uses computation to automatically execute these tasks.
- It's important to note that maintaining privacy often means making sure that all parties are certain that all applications, processes, and frameworks are subjected to an individual verification. In order to prevent users and providers from losing trust, operations should stay open and accessible to both users and providers. To promote data usability and to encourage transparency, it is important that all actions are taken, including the compilation, review, downloading, modification, transfer, and distribution of personal data is registered constantly and is accessible to both consumers and service providers.

Numerous scholars spread the idea that privacy and security are synonymous due to their shared philosophical and analytical roots.

To ensure the protection of sensitive data, it is essential to establish a distinct definition of data privacy. This is to avoid the misunderstanding that is created by the assumption that protection has the purpose of preserving and regulating data, while privacy is about making the best possible choices about how to obtain, handle, and disseminate personal data, both of which are regulated by rules, legislation, social standards, contracts, economics, policies, or some combination of the above. From a data privacy safety standpoint, encryption is used to implement decisions but is not itself a way of maintaining privacy. In other words, Cavoukian [54] learned how this concept could be included in the different design viewpoints. The approach is explored and clarified using two case studies; the primary purpose of the first case study is to demonstrate how personal data is processed in risk analysis and compliance testing. The other one aims to systematically analyze privacy risks and potential issues associated with the application of privacy standards and policies within the system, in order to facilitate the adoption of privacy by design and protection in various fields.

Given below is a general overview of the privacy and security compliance for any smart healthcare systems:

- Any information or data obtained must be collected, analyzed, and used equally in compliance with the legislation.
- Both data must be managed and used with an appropriate degree of confidentiality and privacy rights.
- Connected IoT devices must be capable of sending and receiving data while maintaining data consistency and integrity.
- Clear and Unambiguous Data Collection, Transfer, Usage, and Consent Procedures: Protocols that handle sensitive data, its transmission, authorized access, and informed decisions, must be simple and unambiguous. With the new knowledge, the patients will have more confidence, and the responsibility for their data will be explicitly spelled out so that transparency will be seen quickly.

When making decisions on what minimal security criteria are needed to safeguard data in a smart health environment, It is often necessary to consider the bare minimum security, privacy, and device specifications.

7.2.3 Solutions to Privacy and Security Challenges

This section introduces the privacy and security tools already applied for advanced smart healthcare applications. Such programs would have a massive effect on healthcare investment, protection, privacy, dependability, and trust. While researchers work hard, it is also important to devote extra time to addressing privacy and security problems in smart e-Health systems so that progress can be achieved. In addition, it often includes identifying new flaws and devising reliable countermeasures that will boost the system's overall privacy and security.

On the basis of issues discussed in the previous section, the key solutions can be categorized by addressing the authentication and access control of any smart healthcare system.

7.3 Authentication

When it comes to smart health system architecture, distinguishing genuine people and artifacts is important. Due to the technological characteristics of smart-health applications, it is important to employ both user and device authentication. The widespread use of technology such as radio frequency identification (RFID) has made it possible to distinguish real objects and individuals in commonplace environments. An authentication technology that uses centralized processing can be described as a centralized authentication technology, while an authentication technology that uses decentralized processing is defined as a decentralized authentication technology.

7.3.1 Authentication through Smart Devices

It is possible to assemble thousands of interconnected devices in a smart healthcare system. Due to this, authentication plays a vital security mechanism, as it helps to identify and validate users/devices in wireless networks. RFID is widely employed in smart healthcare devices too and can be identified using a unique serial number stored inside a microchip. It has the advantage of being able to read information without making physical contact. This illustration from Figure 7.9 depicts an RFID-enabled smart healthcare system with two distinct modules: the RFID sensing module that contains RFID

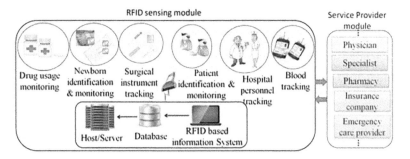

Figure 7.9   RFID-enabled smart healthcare monitoring system [55].

identification and monitoring devices, and a service provider module that contains mechanisms to implement secure identification of users. The RFID sensing module is used to send patients' data to a specific monitoring system, such as an alarm device that will be triggered in the event of an emergency.

Concerns around RFID-based healthcare services derive from the need to ensure that consumer identity is maintained as RFID recognition data is used. With this in mind, it was proposed by Rahman et al. [55] that in order to keep unwanted leaks of confidential health information at bay, a healthcare service access management system should be introduced that incorporates access control strategies. To demonstrate in Figure 7.10, by using writing and privacy policy set by an "Administrator," data access and usage can be directly linked to different data policies specified by the user. A "Privacy Policy Manager" helps to split privacy policies into unique

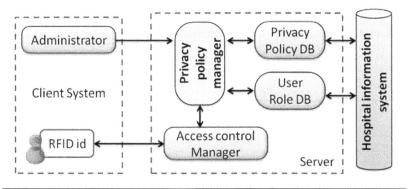

Figure 7.10   Access control management by defining privacy policies [55].

policies and unit functions, and they are all held in separate databases called "Privacy Policy Database" and "User Role Database" in order to provide security against real-time RFID tags that have been scanned into the device.

7.3.2 Authentication through Electrocardiogram Signals

Biometric security has improved tremendously in IoT-enabled applications, owing to which there is a growth in the use of it. In comparison to using standard passwords, which can be easily forgotten, biometric data such as fingerprints, facial expressions, and other facial data can be used as a robust way to authenticate users to different smart devices. Biometric authentication can also be used in mobile phones for validating users like Apple's touch ID or Android's face unlock feature. After creating a new authentication scheme based on fingerprint data, the use of the fingerprint data is applied in user registration and secure user access control. Almost all healthcare systems use an ECG to track and register their system-generated cardiac electrical activity signals, and hence, ECG-based authentication is used for user authentication and for health-related data [56]. It is likely that integrating machine learning algorithms into the patient biometric-processing framework could improve the user authentication process. Another way to put it is, as seen in Figure 7.11, a generic system shows how ECG signals can identify the individual (patient). To a large degree, these measures cover topics like data selection, preprocessing, attribute extraction, and classification-based identification. After a lot of work on cleaning the ECG signals, feature vectors were effectively extracted from the cleaned ECG signals, which in turn could then be used to train a decision model. Based on the assessment, it can be

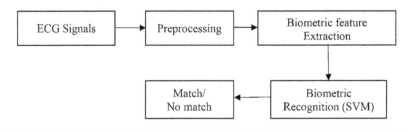

Figure 7.11 Electrocardiogram (ECG)-based user authentication [56].

deduced that SVM-based classification technique for facial recognition gives the most optimal testing outcomes.

7.3.3 Authentication through Attribute-Based Encryption

As healthcare organizations expand in size, different types of attributes may be incorporated into the security architecture. For instance, ciphertext policy-attribute-based encryption (CP-ABE) is being tested for safe communication in SHSs, while key-policy attribute-based encryption (KP-ABE) is also under consideration. In the words of Ambrosin et al. (2016) [57], a hidden key reflects access policies in the KP-ABE (knowledge-protected-but-audit-accessible) mode. As a result, users can decrypt the cyphertext to check whether the given access policy linked with the secret key can be fulfilled by given attributes. The CP-ABE method is the opposite of the CP-PLA method: Instead of imposing access policies on records, it assigns attributes to the hidden key. To make matters worse, this also allows the user the right to decode the cyphertext when the access policies on the plaintext match the key.

Public key infrastructures (PKIs) will underpin various stable, collaborative networks that are based on trust relations among certified authorities (CAs). Figure 7.12 is a generic example of a PKI authentication case. With a CA generating/issuing a key certificate, clients can connect safely by exchanging public keys for encryption

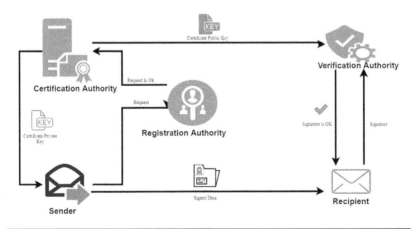

Figure 7.12   Public Key Infrastructure (PKI) example [58].

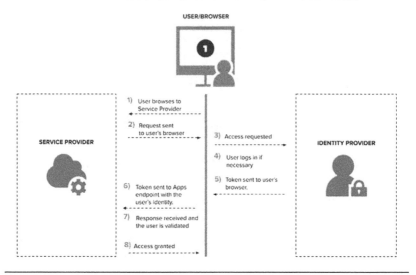

Figure 7.13   Illustration for Single Sign On (SSO) procedure.

and restricting encrypted information to private key owners. For the vast majority of organizations, hierarchical confidence is found to be better and usually leads to a high CA involvement (Perl, 1999). Hierarchies typically represent different protection levels, each of which needs some CAs to react.

SSO has been widely implemented to eliminate the need for legitimate users to repeatedly authenticate with potentially remote services. To execute this, customize the *Shibboleth* device, as seen in Figure 7.13. Service provider (SP), identity provider (IdP), and the "where-are-you-from" (WAYF) service are all required in the SSO process [59]. When the SP receives an access request, it directs the requestor to one of the WAYF services. This allows the user to choose an identity provider to check the identity. As partnerships between organizations develop, requests from specific client locations should be authenticated using local authentication at their home locations, allowing them to sign in and use multiple services (hosted by different SPs).

7.3.4 Access Control Mechanism

Access control mechanisms are mainly used to determine who has the authority to access data and make use of resources. In healthcare, conventional access control only marginally serves the needs.

Following the introduction of surveillance, a patient-saving emergency access management paradigm is now required in certain risky situations. In addition, different patient-centered approaches are discussed in smart healthcare. Re-establishing data management in the hands of patients would have a strong motivating impact on their involvement in various health-related programs.

7.3.5 Patient-Centric Access Control

When (patients) are accessing healthcare facilities, they plan to use, store, and share their confidential health records with their trusted providers. Current systems often give control to users in order to allow them to use various services. This is where it is critical to rely on authentication and authorization methods that are applied to the user in order to handle secure data management. When considering OpenID and OAuth, they can be used together to allow users to have access to multiple websites or services with a single login and identify whether to accept special operations on infrastructure and then generate access tokens.

This principle is illustrated in Figure 7.14; the method will consist of one or more of the following: a user, an OP (OpenID provider), and an RP (replaying party) [60]. This acts as a base for OAuth, which allows clients, owners of resources, servers that manage resources, and authorization servers to be merged together. With this being said, it is a function that is in place and resource servers can release details only when the client shows their permission tokens, which are received from the authorization server.

7.3.6 Role-Based Access Control

Role-based access control (RBAC) makes access control simpler by offering responsibilities and permissions (Gilbert, 1995) [61,62]. In recent years, RBAC has been more commonly used in e-health systems due to its simplicity (Sahi et al.) [19]. For instance, a health attendant (e.g., nurse) may use the writing privilege to insert medical information into the healthcare database, as seen in Figure 7.15. In fact, there are only a couple of healthcare cases where reading is not required. Since their work requirements necessitate them to study all

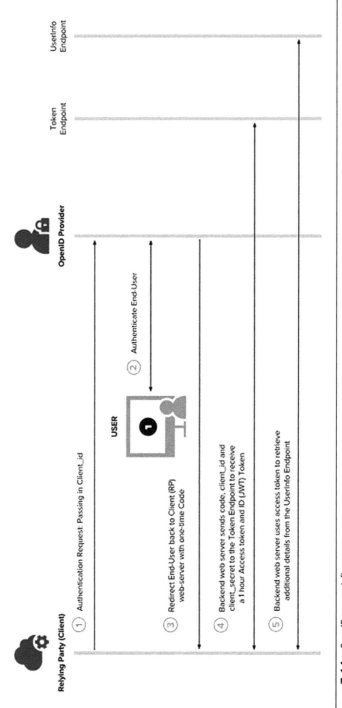

Figure 7.14 OpenID connect flow.

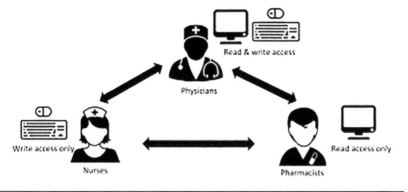

Figure 7.15   Role-based access control in smart healthcare systems [19].

experimental drugs prior to delivering them to patients, pharmacists and doctors alike need to perform similar research before prescribing medication to patients. Additionally, it is the case that there are a variety of approaches made to fill the requirements that come from ethical and legitimate sources, for example, applying access control models to help clinical care and study.

7.3.7 Context-Aware Access Control

A smart healthcare–based e-Health system is capable of deciding what sort of assistance the patient really needs only if they have a complete and accurate picture of the patient's condition. Because of the advances in e-Health services, we require that contextual data is correctly understood in order to achieve an equitable interpretation of data that covers the full meaning of a patient's or caregiver's situation or on the needs of a health professional. Due to data acquisition and data processing problems like context-based services and information, and the interpretation of context-based services and information, it's difficult to include context-awareness in smart healthcare systems. One excellent example of this theory can be seen in the implementation of context-aware control systems. These kinds of systems need to account for how the patient's situation is perceived whether by clinical or physiological influences. Another essential aspect of a system is to take into account all of the related contextual variables, including human actions, artifacts, place, time, frequency, and mood [61]. The medical history as well as all available historical evidence such as medical reports of disorders, diagnosis, recovery plans, and everyday actions should be taken into consideration.

7.3.8 Anonymity

The protection of personal privacy is considered a personal privilege that must be ensured. However, unwanted disclosures of patient characteristics can be introduced for surveillance programs. In addition to patient needs, standards specified in ethical and legitimate legislation must be fulfilled during data exchange. While health databases are released for testing purposes, one of the most preferred instances is to maintain participants' identity anonymous (Harrelson & Falletta) [60]. When it comes to health data analytics, it's necessary to balance the preservation of thresholds and information leakage with modifications to initial concepts intended to anonymize.

For less anonymity, the use of statistical disclosure control (SDC) provides data usefulness while also preserving the confidentiality of attributes that could be recognizable and/or non-identifiable (Shlomo) [63]. As seen in Figure 7.16, a risk-utility is used to demonstrate the trade-off that occurs between data utility and disclosure risk: Given a maximum acceptable risk ratio that's appropriate to data

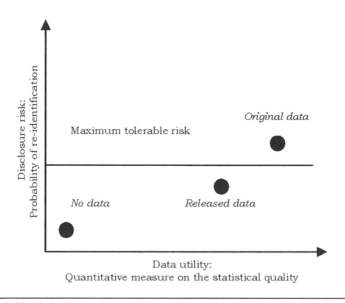

Figure 7.16   Risk-utility confidentiality map [63].

custodians (such as hospitals) and data subjects (such as patients), the most effective SDC approach will have to reduce the amount of information leakage.

7.4 Conclusion and Discussion on Open Research Issues for Future

Smart healthcare platforms are revolutionary technologies with large implementations that can be incorporated into almost any device. A lot of policymakers and *Fortune* 500 businesses are either investigating or have already begun adopting and applying this technology. It is important to design privacy and security mechanisms as health-related practices are being introduced with information and communications technology (ICT). Much of the recent literature on security, access management, and anonymization should guarantee that people have access to their health records while a variety of specialized considerations relating to "smart features" can be discussed as well. In terms of consumer trust being inextricably intertwined with both the quality and privacy of service, this chapter critically explores protection and privacy-preserving technologies designed in the framework of smart healthcare and reviews the applications' ability to meet privacy needs as well as their ability to improve service quality in a data-rich environment.

In order to implement smart healthcare–based computing in an e-Health environment, particular problems unique to the integration and application of these technologies must be addressed.

- Given the amount of data we need to process to get specifics on home amenities, traffic, medical care, and human knowledge, our data processing approaches must be light in order to deliver quick, smooth, and constant services. Healthcare is one of the most intimate and sensitive information exchanges in real life. Encryption is paramount in providing patient safety and protection when sharing patient information between different channels. It provides patient confidentiality and honesty at a low computing rate.
- Any consumer wants custom apps according to their specific needs based on their personal objectives, job place, company type, and other different information. In certain instances,

the expectations of the people are relatively straightforward to fulfill, but in other situations, it is more complicated. Workflows differ according to the situation. Thus, either IoT or cloud storage is more appropriate based on what needs to be achieved. However, it is beneficial to have flexibility and efficiency, all of which occur as a result of being combined with a cloud-based environment.

- Data collection through IoT sensors and other IoT technologies is frequently required as a security practice in smart cities. Although most healthcare systems use sensors to access patient information, which is then used for data processing and analytics. Nonetheless, much of the information available like this will certainly contain private data and sensitive personal characteristics, and so the implications of such data leaking are all too real. It is not just private data that can be anonymized by such measures; other government regulations that are set out to encourage greater transparency and improve the balance between gains and security risks can also be implemented.

- The design of smart healthcare systems depends on the sensors used to access the environment in which various security threats occur. This is why it is important to develop a threat-assessment system. This will be helpful to those patients who chose to use the offered facilities. Because of the collection of information obtained by sensors, it is difficult to build a knowledge model that incorporates all of the potential threats and other considerations that are important in the risk assessment. Besides, designing appropriate strategies for minimizing each paradigm is time-consuming. Hence, to ensure privacy and security in smart healthcare systems, a combination of these technologies can be considered.

References

1. Nguyen, Lemai, Emilia Bellucci, and Linh Thuy Nguyen. "Electronic health records implementation: An evaluation of information system impact and contingency factors." *International Journal of Medical Informatics* 83, no. 11 (2014): 779–796.

2. Solanas, Agusti, Constantinos Patsakis, Mauro Conti, Ioannis S. Vlachos, Victoria Ramos, Francisco Falcone, Octavian Postolache, et al. "Smart health: A context-aware health paradigm within smart cities." *IEEE Communications Magazine* 52, no. 8 (2014): 74–81.

3. Eysenbach, G. "What is e-health." *Journal of Medical Internet Research* 3, no. 2 (2001): e20.

4. Demirkan, Haluk. "A smart healthcare systems framework." *It Professional* 15, no. 5 (2013): 38–45.

5. Amrutha, K. R., S. M. Haritha, Vasu M. Haritha, A. J. Jensy, Sreechithra Sasidharan, and Jomon K. Charly. "IOT based medical home." *International Journal of Computer Applications* 165, no. 11 (2017): 8–14.

6. Prakash, R., and A. Balaji Ganesh. "Internet of things (IoT) enabled wireless sensor network for physiological data acquisition." In *International Conference on Intelligent Computing and Applications*, pp. 163–170. Springer, Singapore, 2019.

7. Pasha, Maruf, and Syed Muhammad Waqas Shah. "Framework for e-health systems in IoT-based environments." *Wireless Communications and Mobile Computing*, 2018 (2018): 1–11.

8. O'Keefe, Christine M., and Chris J. Connolly. "Privacy and the use of health data for research." *Medical Journal of Australia* 193, no. 9 (2010): 537–541.

9. Lowrance, William. "Learning from experience: Privacy and the secondary use of data in health research." *Journal of Health Services Research & Policy* 8, no. 1_suppl (2003): 2–7.

10. Metzger, Andreas, and Clarissa Cassales Marquezan. "Future internet apps: The next wave of adaptive service-oriented systems?" In *European Conference on a Service-Based Internet*, pp. 230–241. Springer, Berlin, Heidelberg, 2011.

11. Provost, Foster, and Tom Fawcett. *Data Science for Business: What You Need to Know about Data Mining and Data-Analytic Thinking*. O'Reilly Media, Inc., 2013.

12. Sakr, Sherif, and Amal Elgammal. "Towards a comprehensive data analytics framework for smart healthcare services." *Big Data Research* 4 (2016): 44–58.

13. Kostadinovska, Ana, Gert-Jan de Vries, Gijs Geleijnse, and Katerina Zdravkova. "Employing personal health records for population health management." In *International Conference on ICT Innovations*, pp. 65–74. Springer, Cham, 2014.

14. Catarinucci, Luca, Danilo De Donno, Luca Mainetti, Luca Palano, Luigi Patrono, Maria Laura Stefanizzi, and Luciano Tarricone. "An IoT-aware architecture for smart healthcare systems." *IEEE Internet of Things Journal* 2, no. 6 (2015): 515–526.

15. Baig, Mirza Mansoor, and Hamid Gholamhosseini. "Smart health monitoring systems: An overview of design and modeling." *Journal of Medical Systems* 37, no. 2 (2013): 1–14.

16. Ghamari, Mohammad, Balazs Janko, R. Simon Sherratt, William Harwin, Robert Piechockic, and Cinna Soltanpur. "A survey on wireless body area networks for e-healthcare systems in residential environments." *Sensors* 16, no. 6 (2016): 831.

17. Khan, Mobeen, Muhammad Taha Jilani, Muhammad Khalid Khan, and M. Bin Ahmed. "A security framework for wireless body area network based smart healthcare system." In *Conference: International Conference for Young Researchers in Informatics, Mathematics and Engineering, ICYRIME*, p. 6, 2017.

18. Gope, Prosanta, and Tzonelih Hwang. "BSN-care: A secure IoT-based modern healthcare system using body sensor network." *IEEE Sensors Journal* 16, no. 5 (2015): 1368–1376.

19. Sahi, Muneeb Ahmed, Haider Abbas, Kashif Saleem, Xiaodong Yang, Abdelouahid Derhab, Mehmet A. Orgun, Waseem Iqbal, Imran Rashid, and Asif Yaseen. "Privacy preservation in e-healthcare environments: State of the art and future directions." *IEEE Access* 6 (2017): 464–478.

20. Ambarkar, Smita Sanjay, and Narendra Shekokar. "Toward Smart and Secure IoT Based Healthcare System." In *Internet of Things, Smart Computing and Technology: A Roadmap Ahead*, pp. 283–303. Springer, Cham, 2020.

21. Farahani, Bahar, Mojtaba Barzegari, Fereidoon Shams Aliee, and Khaja Ahmad Shaik. "Towards collaborative intelligent IoT eHealth: From device to fog, and cloud." *Microprocessors and Microsystems* 72 (2020): 102938.

22. Abouelmehdi, Karim, Abderrahim Beni-Hssane, Hayat Khaloufi, and Mostafa Saadi. "Big data security and privacy in healthcare: A review." *Procedia Computer Science* 113 (2017): 73–80.

23. O'Connor, Yvonne, Wendy Rowan, Laura Lynch, and Ciara Heavin. "Privacy by design: Informed consent and internet of things for smart health." *Procedia Computer Science* 113 (2017): 653–658.

24. Hathaliya, Jigna J., and Sudeep Tanwar. "An exhaustive survey on security and privacy issues in Healthcare 4.0." *Computer Communications* 153 (2020): 311–335.

25. Aceto, Giuseppe, Valerio Persico, and Antonio Pescapé. "Industry 4.0 and health: Internet of things, big data, and cloud computing for healthcare 4.0." *Journal of Industrial Information Integration* 18 (2020): 100129.

26. Butpheng, Chanapha, Kuo-Hui Yeh, and Hu Xiong. "Security and privacy in IoT-cloud-based e-health systems—A comprehensive review." *Symmetry* 12, no. 7 (2020): 1191.

27. Robinson, Y. Harold, X. Arogya Presskila, and T. Samraj Lawrence. "Utilization of Internet of Things in Health Care Information System." In *Internet of Things and Big Data Applications*, pp. 35–46. Springer, Cham, 2020.

28. Shewale, M. A. D., and I. O. T. based Smart. "Secure health care system analysis & data comparison." *International Journal for Research in Applied Science and Engineering Technology* 8, no. 1 (2020): 394–398.

29. Islam, Md Sanju, Fozilatoon Humaira, and Fernaz Narin Nur. "Healthcare applications in IoT." *Global Journal of Medical Research: B Pharma, Drug Discovery, Toxicology & Medicine* 20 (2020): 1–3.

30. Tal, Asher, Zvika Shinar, David Shaki, Shlomi Codish, and Aviv Goldbart. "Validation of contact-free sleep monitoring device with comparison to polysomnography." *Journal of Clinical Sleep Medicine* 13, no. 3 (2017): 517–522.

31. Ray, Partha Pratim, Dinesh Dash, Khaled Salah, and Neeraj Kumar. "Blockchain for IoT-based healthcare: Background, consensus, platforms, and use cases." *IEEE Systems Journal* (2020).

32. Gordon, William J., and Christian Catalini. "Blockchain technology for healthcare: Facilitating the transition to patient-driven interoperability." *Computational and Structural Biotechnology Journal* 16 (2018): 224–230.

33. Sadek, Ibrahim, Edwin Seet, Jit Biswas, Bessam Abdulrazak, and Mounir Mokhtari. "Nonintrusive vital signs monitoring for sleep apnea patients: A preliminary study." *IEEE Access* 6 (2017): 2506–2514.

34. Free icons designed by freepik | flaticon https://www.flaticon.com/authors/freepik

35. Nazir, Shah, Yasir Ali, Naeem Ullah, and Iván García-Magariño. "Internet of things for healthcare using effects of mobile computing: A systematic literature review." *Wireless Communications and Mobile Computing*, 2019 (2019): 1–19.

36. Semantha, Farida Habib, Sami Azam, Kheng Cher Yeo, and Bharanidharan Shanmugam. "A systematic literature review on privacy by design in the healthcare sector." *Electronics* 9, no. 3 (2020): 452.

37. Wu, Jia, Xiaoming Tian, and Yanlin Tan. "Hospital evaluation mechanism based on mobile health for IoT system in social networks." *Computers in Biology and Medicine* 109 (2019): 138–147.

38. Khatoon, Naghma, Sharmistha Roy, and Prashant Pranav. "A Survey on Applications of Internet of Things in Healthcare." In *Internet of Things and Big Data Applications*, pp. 89–106. Springer, Cham, 2020.

39. Aazam, Mohammad, Imran Khan, Aymen Abdullah Alsaffar, and Eui-Nam Huh. "Cloud of things: Integrating internet of things and cloud computing and the issues involved." In *Proceedings of 2014 11th International Bhurban Conference on Applied Sciences & Technology (IBCAST) Islamabad, Pakistan, 14th–18th January 2014*, pp. 414–419. IEEE, 2014.

40. Kang, James Jin, Henry Larkin, J. J. Kang, and H. Larkin. "Intelligent personal health devices converged with internet of things networks." *Journal of Mobile Multimedia* 12, no. 3&4 (2017): 197–212.

41. Wang, Xiaonan, and Shaohao Cai. "Secure healthcare monitoring framework integrating NDN-based IoT with edge cloud." *Future Generation Computer Systems* 112 (2020): 320–329.

42. Yamin, Mohammad. "IT applications in healthcare management: A survey." *International Journal of Information Technology* 10, no. 4 (2018): 503–509.

43. Ismail, Yasser, ed. *Internet of Things (IoT) for Automated and Smart Applications*. BoD–Books on Demand, 2019.

44. Cha, Shi-Cho, Tzu-Yang Hsu, Yang Xiang, and Kuo-Hui Yeh. "Privacy enhancing technologies in the internet of things: Perspectives and challenges." *IEEE Internet of Things Journal* 6, no. 2 (2018): 2159–2187.

45. Zhou, Jun, Zhenfu Cao, Xiaolei Dong, and Athanasios V. Vasilakos. "Security and privacy for cloud-based IoT: Challenges." *IEEE Communications Magazine* 55, no. 1 (2017): 26–33.

46. Cherdantseva, Yulia, and Jeremy Hilton. "A reference model of information assurance & security." In *2013 International Conference on Availability, Reliability and Security*, pp. 546–555. IEEE, 2013.

47. Aldowah, Hanan, Shafiq Ul Rehman, and Irfan Umar. "Security in internet of things: Issues, challenges and solutions." In *International Conference of Reliable Information and Communication Technology*, pp. 396–405. Springer, Cham, 2018.

48. Sadek, Ibrahim, Shafiq Ul Rehman, Josué Codjo, and Bessam Abdulrazak. "Privacy and security of IoT based healthcare systems: Concerns, solutions, and recommendations." In *International Conference on Smart Homes and Health Telematics*, pp. 3–17. Springer, Cham, 2019.

49. Kalyani, G., and Shilpa Chaudhari. "An efficient approach for enhancing security in internet of things using the optimum authentication key." *International Journal of Computers and Applications* 42, no. 3 (2020): 306–314.

50. Yu, Yicheng, Liang Hu, and Jianfeng Chu. "A secure authentication and key agreement scheme for IoT-based cloud computing environment." *Symmetry* 12, no. 1 (2020): 150.

51. García, Laura, Lorena Parra, Jose M. Jimenez, Jaime Lloret, and Pascal Lorenz. "IoT-based smart irrigation systems: An overview on the recent trends on sensors and IoT systems for irrigation in precision agriculture." *Sensors* 20, no. 4 (2020): 1042.

52. Wong, Richmond Y., and Deirdre K. Mulligan. "Bringing design to the privacy table: Broadening "design" in "privacy by design" through the lens of HCI." In *Proceedings of the 2019 CHI Conference on Human Factors in Computing Systems*, pp. 1–17, 2019.

53. Garg, Arpan, and Nitin Mittal. "A Security and Confidentiality Survey in Wireless Internet of Things (IoT)." In *Internet of Things and Big Data Applications*, pp. 65–88. Springer, Cham, 2020.

54. Cavoukian, Ann, and Jeff Jonas. *Privacy by Design in the Age of Big Data*. Information and Privacy Commissioner of Ontario, Canada, 2012.

55. Rahman, Farzana, Md Zakirul Alam Bhuiyan, and Sheikh Iqbal Ahamed. "A privacy preserving framework for RFID based healthcare systems." *Future Generation Computer Systems* 72 (2017): 339–352.

56. Hejazi, Maryamsadat, Syed Abdul Rahman Al-Haddad, Yashwant Prasad Singh, Shaiful Jahari Hashim, and Ahmad Fazli Abdul Aziz. "ECG biometric authentication based on non-fiducial approach using kernel methods." *Digital Signal Processing* 52 (2016): 72–86.

57. Ambrosin, Moreno, Arman Anzanpour, Mauro Conti, Tooska Dargahi, Sanaz Rahimi Moosavi, Amir M. Rahmani, and Pasi Liljeberg. "On the feasibility of attribute-based encryption on internet of things devices." *IEEE Micro* 36, no. 6 (2016): 25–35.

58. Perlman, Radia. "An overview of PKI trust models." *IEEE Network* 13, no. 6 (1999): 38–43.

59. Chadwick, David W., and Kaniz Fatema. "A privacy preserving authorisation system for the cloud." *Journal of Computer and System Sciences* 78, no. 5 (2012): 1359–1373.

60. Harrelson, John M., and John M. Falletta. "The privacy rule (HIPAA) as it relates to clinical research." *Cancer Clinical Trials: Proactive Strategies* (2007): 199–207.

61. Ferraiolo, David F., Dennis M. Gilbert, and Nickilyn Lynch. "An examination of federal and commercial access control policy needs." In *NIST-NCSC National Computer Security Conference*, pp. 107–116, 1995.

62. Elmisery, Ahmed M., Seungmin Rho, and Mohamed Aborizka. "A new computing environment for collective privacy protection from constrained healthcare devices to IoT cloud services." *Cluster Computing* 22, no. 1 (2019): 1611–1638.

63. Shlomo, Natalie. "Statistical disclosure control methods for census frequency tables." *International Statistical Review* 75, no. 2 (2007): 199–217.

8

FUSION OF INFORMATION THEORETICAL MODELS WITH PERSONALIZED DIFFERENTIAL PRIVACY TO MINIMIZE PRIVACY LOSS IN HEALTHCARE CYBER PHYSICAL SYSTEMS

MANAS KUMAR YOGI[1] AND
A.S.N. CHAKRAVARTHY[2]

[1]CSE Dept., Pragati Engineering
College (A), India
[2]CSE Dept., JNTUK Kakinada, India

Abstract

Information theory models are based on probability theory and statistics features. Information theory often concerns itself with measures of information of the distributions associated with random variables. Important quantities of information are entropy, a measure of information in a single random variable, and mutual information, a measure of information in common between two random variables. We use this robustness of information theory models with personalized differential privacy framework. Personalized differential privacy involves feature of Laplace noise addition based on the individual privacy preferences. By fusion of these two models, we show that our proposed approach reduces the privacy loss and also maintains a calculated balance between privacy, utility, and risk of losing sensitive information of the user. The experimental results in our study show that our fusion model edges past in performance against the most popular methods to preserve privacy of patients in

DOI: 10.1201/9781003269168-8

the cyber-physical ecosystem. The performance metrics used to judge the privacy preservation models are quite reasonable as they offer a significant balance between the various trades-offs occurring during information release from the privacy models.

8.1 Introduction

As indicated by Cisco Internet Business Solutions Group the Internet of Things (IoT) started at some point somewhere in the range of 2008 and 2009 when the quantity of "things or articles" associated with the Internet surpassed the quantity of individuals associated with it. Distributed references to Medical Internet of Things (MIoT) in all likelihood began somewhere in the range of 2012 and 2013 [1]. In 2012, the Government Accounting Office (GAO) suggested in the August release of its Highlights report to Congress that the FDA ought to "create and execute an arrangement growing its emphasis on data security gambles." Indeed, in 2013, the Food and Drug Administration (FDA) gave medical gadget producers direction for the network safety of medical IoT devices, which addressed the organization's "current reasoning on this point." The healthcare area has rushed to integrate MIoT into clinical tasks as increase proficiency, developed activities, cost investment funds and in particular, worked on persistent results [2,3]. Models where MIoT is utilized incorporate circulatory strain and glucose level checking, beat oxymeters, weight/BMI scales, thermometers, spirometers, and EKG observing. The way to progress of MIoT (as a matter of fact, all IoT) is Internet network and the capacity of MIoT gadgets to communicate (patient) data.

The healthcare area is represented by the arrangements of HIPAA and HITECH [4]. Both contain explicit guidelines and/or prerequisites for the security of ePHI and other delicate data. Any cycle, framework, or gadget used to make, send, or store ePHI is dependent upon these arrangements [5]. For medical services associations and suppliers, MIoT gadgets address a few network safety and security insurance challenges, vital to which is that MIoT gadgets don't act, work, or act in similar way as conventional IT gadgets. This distinction is because of a MIoT gadget's center capability of sensing (recovering and communicating data about this present reality and sending it) and actuating (making changes to the actual world). A portion of the distinctions among MIoT and conventional IT include:

1. The capacity to arrange, update, and screen
2. Absence of straightforwardness (black box issue)
3. Similarity with existing infrastructure
4. Data security (CIA)
5. Outsider access

The capacity to design, update, and screen implies, at any rate, approaching the MIoT gadget to perform routine and case-by-case administration works, for example, access control (e.g., passwords), software refreshes (i.e., fix the board), and log survey [6]. Because of assembling plan and creation, this degree of access may not be accessible or even conceivable. It may not be imaginable to be aware, to a healthy level of confidence, on the off chance that the MIoT gadget is working appropriately or by any means. Absence of straightforwardness (black box issue) is an issue with a MIoT gadget because of their plan and production. Such gadgets don't permit knowledge into their design, functional settings, or execution/movement logs. Absence of straightforwardness forestalls typical or routine network safety and security assurance oversight, and brings risk into an IT climate since the condition of consistence (with HIPAA/HITECH guidelines) is mysterious. Similarity with existing infrastructures might cause worry for laid out data centers and IT organizations. Since MIoT gadgets might work and work uniquely in contrast to conventional IT gadgets, such distinction can bring about contradiction with frameworks that were not intended for a MIoT mix [7,8]. Thus, MIoT gadgets might require new administration frameworks for legitimate activity and oversight with IT departments tracking down its importance to add assets (staff and abilities or outer administrations) to oversee MIoT sending inside their organizations.

Data security (CIA) is a center occupant of HIPAA. CIA implies finding a way suitable ways to safeguard the confidentiality, integrity and availability of safeguarded well-being data [9]. In the event that a MIoT gadget stores information (not all do), it is important that it be secured – contingent upon whether said data is utilizing cryptography or a few different methods for information insurance. "Discovery" gadgets or gadgets with no kind of access or understanding into their activity or status present critical gambles in the case of exploit or split the difference [10,11].

Outsider access is of worry for MIoT gadgets, which license no closure client admittance to their setup settings or functional status (just outsiders). Such "unmanaged" gadgets might forestall continuous access during a functional mistake or disappointment with access postponed further assuming the outsider is inaccessible. It might likewise forestall those mindful from appropriately measuring organization or functional status of a MIoT gadget when a software or firmware update is required, a gadget EOL is reached, or for other routine administration and support capabilities [12]. Likewise, a maker's software bill of materials (SBOM) might be inaccessible to a medical services supplier that is thinking about involving MiOT gadgets in its clinical setting(s).

8.2 Current State of Art

Aftercare checking of patients in the wake of being released from a medical clinic and noticing their healing for a suggested period by their doctors in their own space forestalls either missing a basic circumstance that requires sending a premed at home for help or a superfluous reconfirmation. Nonstop well-being and action checking frameworks can be formulated by either surrounding sensors situated in the home, emergency clinic, or rescue vehicle or wearables/implantable conveyed by the patients as they continue on the streets. Various brilliant climate projects with physical testbeds and preliminaries have been executed and the subsequent datasets are accessible for scientists to mine, including the CASAS project, technology integrated health management (TIHM) [13,14], or savvy emergency clinic process digging for the executives. Next to the checking frameworks, the tele-medical procedure is another well-being use case in emergency clinics. Mechanical medical procedure frameworks, (for example, instinctive Da Vinci and Cambridge medical technology) have set the stage for a neighborhood specialist in the activity space to work, utilizing visual and haptic signs and get help from a specialist partner whenever required. Correspondence innovation progressions, for example, 5G URLLC and Tactile Internet (IEEE 1918.1) are planning to furnish a shut circle control highlight with latencies in the scope of milliseconds have empowered telesurgery over a specific remote distance [15].

Nonstop confirmation has built up some decent forward movement as of late because of the expansion of gadgets that empower the assortment of multi-modular biometrics by means of different sensors (like an accelerometer for stride investigation). Notwithstanding, the utilization of persistent verification to help medical care correspondence over non-public organizations has not been adequately investigated. This part depicts the works connecting with gadgets normally utilized in medical services. Cell phones are generally utilized among medical services professionals. The screens on cell phones have shown to be rich wellsprings of biometrics in different examinations. In [16] the creators present an original plan for contact motion put together validation with respect to cell phones, accomplishing an equivalent blunder rate (EER) of 0–4%. Composing with keystrokes or signals has additionally been displayed to yield promising biometrics for consistent verification. The consideration of cameras on most current cell phones have prompted the acknowledgment of persistent face confirmation. All the more as of late, plans utilizing multimodal ways of behaving have been created to utilize the client climate (e.g., Wi-Fi and Bluetooth data) to all the more likely validate. A few plans have utilized comparable biometrics to lay out which access strategy to allow the client; something that can be utilized to give a layered admittance to information in view of the privacy of that information. Workstations and personal computers are additionally consistently utilized in the medical services profession for the info and access of data. A famous keystroke study was presented in [17] with EERs of ~10%. In [18], the creators show mouse development conduct is a doable biometric to confirm. Similarly as with cell phones, the face has likewise been recommended for consistent validation plans on PCs. This segment uncovers that while there have been endeavours made to consistently confirm, such plans have not seen critical application in medical services.

Masking is a strategy of concealing unique information with changed content. Halfway upsides of a cryptographic calculation are randomized by masking, which maintains a strategic distance from conditions between these qualities and the power utilization applied in an algorithmic level. Also, it doesn't depend on the power utilization qualities of the medical gadget. Scientists proposed a key masking strategy as a software arrangement against DPA assaults. Albeit this strategy endeavors to randomize the mystery key before every execution of the scalar increase, power above is a worry here for medical services gadgets. A bandpass filter [19] or a current-flattening circuit [19] can be added to the cryptosystem to stifle data spillage through the current stock pin. An inside created irregular cover in view of ring oscillators was proposed in [20] to progressively change the power utilization.

8.3 Proposed Approach

For our proposed research, we introduce the utility theory of information. In this concerned theory, the quality of information is the metric to measure of information. We introduce the fusion of personalized differential privacy along with the utility theory of information. We propose a mechanism, in which each user of the system can choose the limit up to which their privacy level can be revealed. Beyond that limit, the sensitive and private information of the user cannot be released.

According to the basic concept involved in utility theory of information, if I_p is the portion of information, then the quality of this information equals probability $P(S,gl)$ where gl denotes the goal of the system S. In our approach, the goal of the system is to limit the release of private information. The main motivation to use utility theory in our proposal is that it helps in determining whether the users' privacy choice behavior is rational or not. For instance, consider privacy choices (named as PCh1, PCh2, ... etc.), if a user prefers PCh1 over PCh2 and PCh2 over PCh3 then the user will prefer PCh1 over PCh3.

When a user, U, has a limited number of privacy alternatives, then the numerical utilities $u(x)$, $u(y)$ ... . etc. can be modeled in a comparative way such that $u(x)$ is not greater than $u(y)$. Now we formulate the trade-off between data privacy and data utility functions using utility differences and even chance alternatives. In the context of even chance, consider we prefer a 50–50 trade-off between data privacy and data utility, then we can represent the utility differences as given by the below equations.

$$1/2u(0) + 1/2u(100) > 1/2u(10) + 1/2u(50) \qquad (8.1)$$

or

$$u(0) + u(100) > u(100) + u(50) \qquad (8.2)$$

or

$$u(100) - u(50) > u(10) - u(0) \qquad (8.3)$$

A decision resulting in maximum expected utility also derives the probability of making the decision preferable up to a certain limit. To fix the upper bound on this limit of privacy, we integrate the notion of personal differential privacy into the utility theory. If datasets D1 and D2 differ with respect to a certain record rd, then

$$D1 - D2 = rd \qquad (8.4)$$

Subsequently, the privacy utility difference becomes P(S,gl)/rd.

The more the rd value decreases, the value of Private data release (PDR) will increase. Naturally our goal is to make rd value more, such that if the P(S,gl) value becomes approximately equal to rd value, then the PDR value will also become closer to 1.

We can now formulate the privacy sensitivity factor (PSF) as a composition of PDR with utility function values, as depicted below.

$$PSF = (PDR) \ \min \ (u(D1), u(D2)) \qquad (8.5)$$

In Equation (8.5), u(D1) and u(D2) are minimum values of private data release for all the records of dataset D1 and D2. Naturally, min (u(D1),u(D2)) will help in reducing the final value of PSF.

8.4 Experimental Results

Figure 8.1 denotes a graph between PDR and PSF. We can observe that they are directly proportional to each other. As the value of PDR increases, the value of PSF too increases. Additionally we can observe that up to a PDR metric value of 8, the percentage growth in PSF is nearly 4%, but when the PDR value increases up to 10, then there is a steep rise in percentage growth of PSF. It represents the fact that to maintain a steady rate of growth in PSF, the PDR value must be controlled.

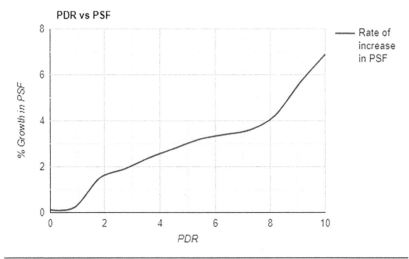

Figure 8.1 Plot between PDR and PSF.

Figure 8.2 denotes the decreasing nature of PDR when there is not much difference in the records between two datasets. To maintain the datasets nearly similar, we need some mechanisms to add noise into the records of the datasets such that the attackers cannot distinguish between the two datasets. Anonymization is the method involved with transforming information into a structure that doesn't

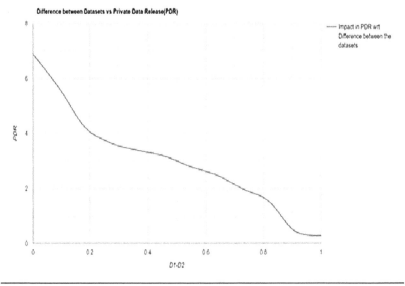

Figure 8.2 Plot of difference between datasets versus PDR.

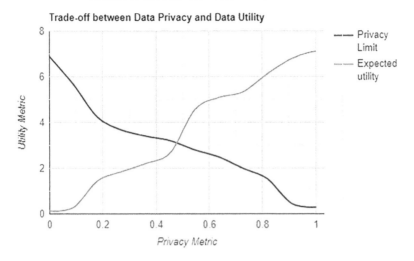

Figure 8.3   Plot between privacy metric and utility metric.

distinguish people. Since sociology is worried about society and human conduct, an anonymization technique to safeguard the character of members is basic to moral examination. Similarly as with assent, arranging anonymization prior to undertaking information assortment produces both informed assent and a less asset course of information anonymization.

The plot in Figure 8.3 represents the trade-off between privacy and utility, which is a long-lasting argument among the design community of any secure system. As shown in the graph above, the intersection point between the two curves of privacy limit and expected utility meet at a point where the ideal trade-off can be maintained. But to maintain this configuration, the assumptions made while designing a secure CPS will also be more. So, for the researchers, it is always difficult to maintain the balance between privacy and data utility. We can observe that the utility metric and privacy metric are inversely related to each other. So, by reducing the data utility to 50%, we can provide nearly 50% of privacy, which may be acceptable in general cases. Nevertheless in healthcare CPS where the cost is patient health and well-being, data utility can be compromised at the cost of increased privacy.

To show that our novel approach performs better than popular methods of privacy in healthcare CPS, we have considered a lung cancer dataset from Kaggle. There are 16 attributes and 284 instances

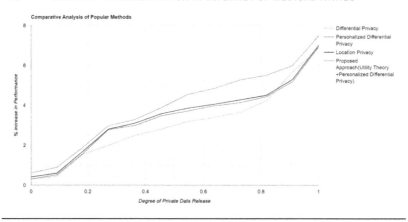

Figure 8.4   Comparative analysis of popular methods.

of patients. In Figure 8.5, we have shown a portion of the dataset. We can add noise to the dataset so that the exact age of the patient and gender also cannot be identified correctly.

From Figure 8.4, we can observe that our proposed approach outperforms current popular methods by at least 2% in performance. Currently, differential privacy is considered to be the best technique to enhance privacy in CPS but it is computationally expensive. For the same reason, our approach makes design optimizations while advocating a robust principle of utility theory. The fusion of personalized differential privacy adds the element of flexibility for the user to limit the degree of privacy as per context. This increase in the degree of flexibility overcomes the computational complexity and helps in reducing the overall cost of the technique.

8.5 Future Directions

We have made certain unavoidable assumptions while designing our novel approach. The first and foremost assumption we made is regarding the nature of user query to the system. We have considered that the queries are simple and correlated. Even if the user inputs nested queries, they are converted into a form that is understandable to the system to release the data with respect to minimum privacy loss. The main drawback results from this approach are that data utility may be limited. So, in order to maintain the trade-off between

	A	B	C	D	E	F	G	H	I	J	K	L	M	N	O	P
1	GENDER	AGE	SMOKING	YELLOW_ FINGERS	ANXIETY	PEER_PRESSU RE	CHRONIC	FATIGUE	ALLERGY	WHEEZING	ALCOHOL	COUGHING	SHORTNESS (	SWALLOWI	CHEST PAIN	LUNG_CANCER
2	M	69	1	2	2	1	1	2	1	2	2	2	2	2	2	YES
3	M	74	2	1	1	1	2	2	2	1	1	1	2	2	2	YES
4	F	59	1	1	1	2	1	2	1	2	1	2	2	1	2	NO
5	M	63	2	2	2	1	1	1	1	1	2	1	1	2	2	NO
6	F	63	1	2	1	1	1	1	1	2	1	2	2	1	1	NO
7	F	75	1	2	1	1	2	2	2	2	1	2	2	1	1	YES
8	M	52	2	1	1	1	1	2	1	2	2	2	2	1	2	YES
9	F	51	2	2	2	2	1	2	2	1	1	1	2	2	1	YES
10	F	68	2	1	2	1	1	2	1	1	1	1	1	1	1	NO
11	M	53	2	2	2	2	2	1	2	1	2	1	1	2	2	YES
12	F	61	2	2	2	2	2	2	1	2	1	2	2	2	1	YES
13	M	72	1	1	1	1	2	2	2	2	2	2	2	1	2	YES
14	F	60	2	1	1	1	1	2	1	1	1	1	2	1	1	NO
15	M	58	2	1	1	1	1	2	2	2	2	2	2	1	2	YES
16	M	69	2	1	1	1	1	1	2	2	2	2	1	1	2	NO
17	F	48	1	2	2	2	2	2	2	2	1	2	2	2	1	YES
18	M	75	2	1	1	1	2	1	2	2	2	2	2	1	2	YES
19	M	57	2	2	2	2	2	1	1	1	2	1	1	2	2	YES
20	F	68	2	2	2	2	2	2	1	1	1	2	2	1	1	YES
21	F	61	1	1	1	1	2	2	1	1	1	1	2	1	1	NO
22	F	44	2	2	2	2	2	2	1	1	1	1	2	2	1	YES
23	F	64	1	2	2	2	1	1	2	2	1	2	1	2	1	YES
24	F	21	2	1	1	1	2	2	2	1	1	1	2	1	1	NO
25	M	60	2	1	1	1	1	2	2	2	2	2	2	1	2	YES
26	M	72	2	2	2	2	2	1	2	2	2	2	1	2	2	YES
27	M	65	1	2	2	1	1	2	1	2	2	2	2	2	2	YES
28	F	61	2	2	2	1	1	2	2	1	2	1	2	2	2	YES

survey lung cancer

Figure 8.5 Portion of dataset used for proposed approach.

utility and privacy, the second assumption is made. This assumption is that the noise is added to the records of the original datasets in such a way that it results in anonymization. But the danger of bad anonymization always lurks in the shadows. The third and final assumption we make is of user privacy choices. We assume every privacy choice the user makes is rational in nature. The drawback arising from this assumption is that the irrational privacy preferences can wreak havoc on the system. The probability of a successful attack increases if the goal of the user is irrational privacy preference. As we are involving personalized differential privacy, we give a certain degree of flexibility to the user to select privacy limit, thereby opening a window for setting irrational privacy choices. In future work, we plan to optimize the minimum expected data utility so that above assumptions can be dissolved. Furthermore, we want to eliminate the assumption of irrational privacy preferences by disallowing the user to select privacy choices outside the scope of rational choices of privacy. Healthcare CPS are becoming the backbone of numerous healthcare institutions so the systems must be designed, making few assumptions at the cost of design optimization with respect to privacy elements.

8.6 Conclusion

This paper advocates an approach for reduction in the privacy loss with the help of fusion of the information theory model and personalized differential privacy. The information theory helps in maintaining a balance between data utility and privacy. The principle of personalized differential privacy helps in providing flexibility to the user to select the limit up to which privacy can be released by the CPS. As medical facilities are increasing day by day, the advent of healthcare CPS system warrants the safety of patient data. In case patient data is accessed by a malicious user, the well being of a patient will be easily compromised. In the long run, such a CPS ecosystem will lose trust in the users. Our paper enlightens a novel mechanism that proves to be better than current popular methods of privacy used in healthcare CPS. This paper will serve as a road map to develop further techniques related to reduction in privacy loss in healthcare CPS.

References

[1] X. Li, Q. Xue, and M. C. Chuah, "Casheirs: Cloud assisted scalable hierarchical encrypted based image retrieval system," in Proc. IEEE INFOCOM 2017, pp. 1–9, May 2017.

[2] H. Ebadi, D. Sands, and G. Schneider, "Differential privacy: Now it's getting personal," in Proc. 42Nd Annual ACM SIGPLAN-SIGACT Symposium on Principles of Programming Languages, POPL '15. ACM, 2015.

[3] Q. Xia et al., "Medshare: Trust-less medical data sharing among cloud service providers via blockchain," *IEEE Access*, vol. 5, pp. 14,757–14,767, 2017.

[4] M. Shen et al., "Privacy-preserving support vector machine training over blockchain-based encrypted IoT data in smart cities," *IEEE Internet of Things J.*, 2019.

[5] S. Cha, T. Hsu, Y. Xiang, and K. Yeh, "Privacy enhancing technologies in the internet of things: Perspectives and challenges," *IEEE IoT J.*, vol. 6, no. 2, pp. 2159–2187, 2019.

[6] IT Governance Privacy Team: EU General Data Protection Regulation (GDPR): An Implementation and Compliance Guide-Second edition. IT Governance Publishing, 2017. http://www.jstor.org/stable/j.ctt1trkk7x

[7] Y. Yang, X. Liu, R. H. Deng, et al., "Lightweight sharable and traceable secure mobile health system," *IEEE Transactions on Dependable and Secure Computing*, 2017.

[8] Y. Yang, X. Liu, and R. H. Deng, "Lightweight break-glass access control system for healthcare internet-of-things," *IEEE Transactions on Industrial Informatics*, 2017.

[9] G. Sun, V. Chang, M. Ramachandran, Z. Sun, G. Li, H. Yu, and D. Liao, "Efficient location privacy algorithm for internet of things (IoT) services and applications," *J. Netw. Comput. Appl.*, vol. 89, pp. 3–13, 2017.

[10] G. Sun, Y. Xie, D. Liao, H. Yu, and V. Chang, "User-defined privacy location sharing system in mobile online social networks," *J. Netw. Comput. Appl.*, vol. 86, pp. 34–45, 2017.

[11] M. A. Habib, M. Ahmad, S. Jabbar, S. Khalid, J. Chaudhry, K. Saleem, J. J. P. C. Rodrigues, and M. SayimKhalil, "Security and privacy based access control model for Internet of connected vehicles," *Future Gener. Comput. Syst.*, vol. 97, pp. 687–696, Aug. 2019.

[12] H. Yeh, T. Chen, P. Liu, T. Kim, and H. Wei, "A secured authentication protocol for wireless sensor networks using elliptic curves cryptography," *Sensors*, vol. 11, no. 5, pp. 4767–4779, May 2011.

[13] W. Shi and P. Gong, "A new user authentication protocol for wireless sensor networks using elliptic curves cryptography," *Int. J. Distrib. Sensor Netw.*, vol. 9, no. 4, Apr. 2013, Art. no. 730831.

[14] F. Wu, L. Xu, S. Kumari, X. Li, A. K. Das, M. K. Khan, M. Karuppiah, and R. Baliyan, "A novel and provably secure authentication and key agreement scheme with user anonymity for

global mobility networks," *Secur. Commun. Netw.*, vol. 9, no. 16, pp. 3527–3542, Nov. 2016.

[15] S. Kumari and H. Om, "Authentication protocol for wireless sensor networks applications like safety monitoring in coal mines," *Comput. Netw.*, vol. 104, pp. 137–154, Jul. 2016.

[16] P. Gope and T. Hwang, "A realistic lightweight anonymous authentication protocol for securing real-time application data access in wireless sensor networks," *IEEE Trans. Ind. Electron.*, vol. 63, no. 11, pp. 7124–7132, Nov. 2016.

[17] F. Wu, X. Li, A. K. Sangaiah, L. Xu, S. Kumari, L. Wu, and J. Shen, "A lightweight and robust two-factor authentication scheme for personalized healthcare systems using wireless medical sensor networks," *Future Gener. Comput. Syst.*, vol. 82, pp. 727–737, May 2018.

[18] S. Oueida, M. Aloqaily, and S. Ionescu, "A smart healthcare reward model for resource allocation in smart city," *Multimedia Tools Appl.*, vol. 78, no. 17, pp. 24,573–24,594, Sep. 2018.

[19] F. Al-Turjman, H. Zahmatkesh, and L. Mostarda, "Quantifying uncertainty in internet of medical things and big-data services using intelligence and deep learning," *IEEE Access*, vol. 7, pp. 115,749–115,759, 2019.

[20] S. Otoum, B. Kantarci, and H. Mouftah, "Adaptively supervised and intrusion-aware data aggregation for wireless sensor clusters in critical infrastructures," in Proc. IEEE Int. Conf. Commun. (ICC), pp. 1–6, May 2008.

Index